JEHOVAH OF THE WATCHTOWER

JEHOVAH OF THE WATCHTOWER

By

WALTER R. MARTIN

and

NORMAN H. KLANN

MOODY PRESS

CHICAGO

Revised edition

Scripture quotations are the author's translation of the Greek
and Hebrew, unless otherwise noted.

ISBN: 0-8024-4290-0

Second Printing, 1975

Printed in the United States of America

TO

Jehovah's Witnesses everywhere who need to know the truth and the way to Him who alone is the life, Jesus Christ our Lord.

Contents

Acknowledgments

We wish to express our thanks to Dr. J. Oliver Buswell, Jr., and Dr. Wilber Wallis. We are also deeply indebted to Dr. Frank E. Gaebelein and Dr. Wilbur M. Smith for their aid and encouragement, which they so faithfully supplied to us throughout our research and the subsequent publication. We trust that, as the material presented is considered, the tremendous need for unified Christian action under the guidance of the Spirit of God may be realized and energetically undertaken in these days when both the proclamation and the defense of the faith are of such prime importance.

Foreword

NOT LONG AGO, a woman engaged me in conversation after a church service. Her brother, she explained, had been a member of one of the larger Protestant denominations but had been captivated by the teachings of Jehovah's Witnesses. Was there anything she might read that would enlighten her as to this cult? The incident is typical; many a Christian minister is being told just such a story and asked much the same question. It has been extraordinarily difficult to make suitable recommendations as to reading matter regarding Jehovah's Witnesses, because of the great paucity of material on the movement. The sad paradox has been that this rapidly spreading cult with its over one-half million followers and lavish financial backing has had very little written about it. Orthodox Christians have contented themselves with denouncing it, but practically nothing has been done in the way of logical examination of its background, claims, and teachings.

This situation has now been remedied. The result is that the church owes a debt of gratitude to Professor Walter R. Martin and the Reverend Norman Klann, who have collaborated in this authoritative study. In it, they have done a piece of pioneer research, and they have done it with scholarly competence and logical force. Eschewing hearsay evidence regarding Jehovah's Witnesses, they have gone to the sources, including the headquarters of the cult itself. The result is, so far as I know, the *first full-length portrait and analysis* of the movement to be published.

The authors' conclusions represent a great deal of painstaking investigation of the claims of this cult which is making tragic inroads upon churches. This is true mainly because these churches are not presenting the gospel with spiritual power and compelling relevance. The judgments passed upon the movement in the following pages are notable for patient investigation, careful thinking, and sound biblical and theological knowledge. This book may well be used to deliver many from a cult which is wresting the Scriptures and obscuring the gospel of Christ, which alone is the power of God unto salvation.

FRANK E. GAEBELEIN

Preface

THE PURPOSE OF THIS STUDY is to present in the clearest and most concise form the doctrines of the Watchtower Bible and Tract Society, or "Jehovah's Witnesses." We shall endeavor to expound to the best of our ability and knowledge the teachings of this organization. It is not our desire or aim to injure the feelings of anyone connected with the organization, but simply to compare the teachings of the Society with the doctrines of the Holy Scriptures. We are well aware that the members of the Watchtower reject "man interpreted" versions of the Bible (King James, Douay, etc.), and in order to allay their animosity, we have used copies of the Greek, Hebrew, and Aramaic Scriptures which best represent the original languages in which the Scriptures were written. We have also taken care to include the Watchtower Bible and Tract Society's publication, *The Emphatic Diaglott*, along with their latest efforts entitled, *The New World Translation of the Hebrew Scriptures*, *The New World Translation of the Christian Greek Scriptures*, and *The Kingdom Interlinear Translation of the Greek Scriptures*. Numerous sources have also been consulted, especially the writings of the Society and its principal advocates. The Septuagint version of the Old Testament has likewise been used, since the Society seems partial to its renderings.

We are conscious of the tremendous doctrinal truths and errors which underlie any discussion of theological dogma, and to avoid confusion, have elected to present in detail the principal doctrines and beliefs of Jehovah's Witnesses as fully as possible. We shall then compare those teachings directly with the whole scope of the Scriptures bearing on the doctrines, and thereby hope to place the several teachings in their true light for further study.

It is unfortunately true in a work of this nature that the critical person may claim that the authors have not authenticated their

11

views in the complete light of all the material available. However, we should like to point out that every available source has been consulted in this study, from Nathan H. Knorr, President of the International Bible Students Association and the Watchtower Bible and Tract Society, to such outstanding biblical scholars as the late Dr. Edgar Goodspeed, Dr. J. Oliver Buswell, Jr., former professor of philosophy, Greek, and systematic theology, Covenant College; Dr. Wilber Wallis, former professor of Greek and exegesis at Covenant College; and Dr. G. Douglas Young, professor of Old Testament history, Hebrew, and Aramaic at the American Institute of Holy Land Studies, Mt. Zion, Israel. A great wealth of material was also made available in the literature of the Watchtower publications, for which we are grateful and express our thanks.

Since Jehovah's Witnesses profess to believe in the Bible as the infallible Word of God and their guide in all doctrines, this study will be based entirely upon what the Bible itself teaches, and *not* upon what it is *thought* to teach. We know it is possible to "eisegete" (read into) the Scriptures many ways, but impossible to "exegete" (take out) from them more than one way, at least where cardinal doctrines of the Christian faith are concerned. We have striven to be honest and straightforward in this approach.

As this edition, revised and enlarged, goes forth, we feel a deep sense of gratitude to the Lord for the way in which He has seen fit to bless the ministry of this work; and it is our earnest prayer that it may continue to warn many of the spiritual dangers within the Jehovah's Witnesses movement.

With these thoughts in mind, then, we shall begin our study of Jehovah's Witnesses, in the prayerful hope that they may come to see, through the power of the Holy Spirit, the fullness of Jehovah-God in the person of Jesus Christ.

WALTER R. MARTIN, Director
Christian Research Institute
Visiting Professor of Comparative Religions
Melodyland School of Theology, Anaheim, California
and
NORMAN H. KLANN, Th.B.

1

The History of the Watchtower

CHARLES TAZE RUSSELL was the founder of what is now Jehovah's Witnesses and the energetic administrator that brought about its far-flung organization. The name *Jehovah's Witnesses,* incidentally, was taken at Columbus, Ohio, in 1931, to differentiate between the Watchtower and the true followers of Russell as represented by the Dawn Bible Students and the Layman's Home Missionary Movement. C. T. Russell was born on February 16, 1852, the son of Joseph L. and Anna Eliza Russell, and spent most of his early years in Pittsburgh and Allegheny, Pennsylvania, where at the age of twenty-five, he was manager of several men's furnishings stores.

At an early age, he rejected the doctrine of eternal punishment, due apparently to the severe indoctrination he had received as a Congregationalist, and as a result of this act, entered upon a long and varied career of denunciation aimed at "organized religions." In 1870, at the age of eighteen, Russell organized a Bible class in Pittsburgh, which in 1876 elected him "Pastor" of the group. From 1876 to 1878, the pastor was assistant editor of a small Rochester, New York, monthly magazine, but resigned when a controversy arose over Russell's counter arguments on the atonement of Christ.

Shortly after leaving his position, Russell founded *Zion's Watch Tower* (1879) which is known today as *The Watchtower Announcing Jehovah's Kingdom.* From 6,000 in 1879 to the staggering figure of nearly 180,000,000* as of January 1973, this maga-

---

Awake magazine, the other Watchtower publication, has a yearly circulation of over 170 million copies, and is fast approaching the circulation of *The Watchtower. Awake* is circulated in 27 languages. *The Watchtower* in 73.

zine has grown until it has surpassed even Russell's fondest dreams. In the year 1884, Pastor Russell incorporated Zion's Watch Tower Tract Society at Pittsburgh, Pennsylvania, which in 1886 published the first in a series of seven books (Russell wrote six) entitled, *Studies in the Scriptures.* The sixth volume was published in 1904 and the seventh in 1917 after his death. The seventh volume, *The Finished Mystery,* caused a split in the organization, which culminated in a clean division, the larger group following J. F. Rutherford. The smaller group remained by itself and subsequently became The Dawn Bible Students Association, which sponsors the coast-to-coast radio program, "Frank and Ernest," publishes *The Dawn* magazine (circulation over 30,000 per month) and has its headquarters and publishing plant in East Rutherford, New Jersey. In the end, under Rutherford's leadership, the Society became known as "Jehovah's Witnesses" and survives to this day.

As of January 1973, The Watchtower Bible and Tract Society (founded in 1896), which is the focal point of the organization, operated in more than 207 lands and sponsored kingdom preaching in the United States alone by more than 483,430 Witnesses. The worldwide membership of Jehovah's Witnesses is in excess of 1,600,000, and attendance at its international assemblies has risen to 3,526,000. In 1972, they sponsored 1,146,328 home Bible studies, spent 267,581,120 hours witnessing, and made 121,226,605 back calls on homes they were attempting to convert. The Society's literature is distributed in more than 160 languages, and it has become a great disseminator of propaganda and a challenge to the zeal of every Christian.

In 1908, the headquarters of the movement were transferred to Brooklyn, New York, where property was purchased (17 Hicks Street) and became known as the Brooklyn Tabernacle. Large tracts of property were purchased by the Society on Columbia Heights, as it grew and prospered, until today, whole blocks are in their possession. Among the other things the Society owns are: a large, up-to-date printing plant which has produced more than *two billion* pieces of literature since its inauguration in 1928 and expansions in 1949 and 1957, a modern apartment building, and office quarters; three "Kingdom Farms," which supply food, wood for furniture, and so on; a Bible school, Gilead, which, since its opening in 1943, has sent out approximately 11,000† missionaries of the kingdom; and many more enterprises. All employees in the factory are allowed fourteen dollars a month, receive room and board, and work for nothing; no salaries are paid.

During the years 1942-52, the membership of Jehovah's Witnesses doubled in North America, multiplied fifteen times in South America, twelve times in the Atlantic islands, five times in Asia, seven times in Europe and Africa, and six times in the islands of the Pacific. By 1973 these figures had almost doubled. Such is the evolution of Pastor Russell's "Zion."

Russell continued his teachings until his death on October 31, 1916, aboard a transcontinental train in Texas. The erstwhile pastor had a remarkable life highly colored with legal entanglements, but not without success in his chosen field. The following account is quoted from *The Brooklyn Daily Eagle,* November 1, 1916, and has been inserted at this point to illustrate Russell's character:

> A year after this publication, "The Watchtower," had been established Russell married Maria Ackley in Pittsburgh. She had become interested in him through his teachings, and she helped him in running the Watchtower.
>
> Two years later, in 1881, came "The Watchtower Bible and Tract Society," the agency through which in later years "Pastor" Russell's sermons were published (as advertisements) in newspapers throughout the world. This Society progressed amazingly under the joint administration of husband and wife, but in 1897 Mrs. Russell left her husband. Six years later, in 1903, she sued for separation.
>
> There was much litigation then that was quite undesirable from the "Pastor's" point of view regarding alimony for his wife, but it was settled in 1909 by the payment of $6,036 to Mrs. Russell. The litigation revealed that "Pastor" Russell's activities in the religious field were carried on through several subsidiary societies and that all of the wealth which flowed into him through these societies was under the control of a holding company in which the "Pastor" held $990 of the $1,000 capital and two of his followers the other $10.

---

†The Watchtower also sponsors special classes for women ministers at Gilead.

Thus Russell apparently controlled the entire financial power of the Society and was not accountable to anyone.

The *Eagle* column goes on to say:

> After the "work" had been well started here, "Pastor" Russell's Watchtower publication advertised wheat seed for sale at $1.00 a pound. It was styled "Miracle Wheat," and it was asserted that it would grow five times as much as any other brand of wheat. There were other claims made for the wheat seed, and the followers were advised to purchase it, the proceeds to go to the Watchtower and be used in publishing the "Pastor's" sermons.
>
> The *Eagle* first made public the facts about this new venture of the Russellites and it published a cartoon picturing the "Pastor" and his "Miracle Wheat" in such a way that "Pastor" Russell brought suit for libel, asking $100,000 damages. Government departments investigated the wheat for which $1.00 a pound was asked, and agents of the Government were important witnesses at the trial of the libel suit in January, 1913. The "Miracle Wheat" was low in the Government tests, they said. The *Eagle* won the suit.

Prior to entering court, the *Eagle* had said,

> The *Eagle* goes even further and declares that at the trial it will show that "Pastor" Russell's religious cult is nothing more than a money-making scheme.

The court's decision vindicated the *Eagle's* statement and proved its reliability.

> All during this time the "Pastor's" sermons were being printed in newspapers throughout the world, notably when he made a tour of the world in 1912 and caused accounts to be published in his advertised sermons telling of enthusiastic greetings at the various places he visited. It was shown in many cases that the sermons were never delivered in the places that were claimed.

For the benefit of any Jehovah's Witness who may think that the "Miracle Wheat" fraud is an invention of the "jealous religionists" who are trying to defame the pastor's memory, we document the scandal, trial, and verdict from the *Brooklyn Daily Eagle* (obtainable at the Montague Street branch of the Brooklyn Public Library) as follows:

1. January 1, 1913, pages 1-2. Miracle Wheat Scandal
2. January 22, 1913, page 2. Testimony of Russellite beliefs.
3. January 23, 24, 1913, page 3. Testimony on wheat.
4. January 25, 1913, page 16. Financial statements proving Russell's absolute control, made by Secretary-Treasurer Van Amberg.
5. *Van Amberg's statement,* "We are not responsible to anyone for our expenditures. We are responsible only to God."
6. January 27, 1913, page 3. Government experts testify on "Miracle Wheat" and ascertain beyond doubt that it is not miraculous or overly excellent.
7. January 28, 1913, page 2. Prosecution and Defense sum-up. Russell assailed, but not present to hear it.
8. January 29, 1913, page 16, Russell loses libel suit.‡

The *Eagle* led the fight to expose the hypocrisy of Pastor Russell, and nothing could be more appropriate than their on-the-spot testimony as to his many fraudulent claims.§ The following documentary evidence is taken from the *Brooklyn Daily Eagle,* page 18, February 19, 1912, and is entitled "Pastor Russell's Imaginary Sermons—Printed Reports of Addresses in Foreign Lands that He Never Made—One at Hawaii, a Sample." These excerpts concern the pastor's "world tour" and are very enlightening with respect to his reliability and truthfulness.

> "Pastor" Russell, who has found the atmosphere of Brooklyn uncongenial ever since the *Eagle* published the facts concerning his methods and morals, is making some new records in the far parts of the world. He is delivering sermons to imaginary audiences on tropical islands and completing "searching investigations" into the missions of China and Japan by spending a few hours in each country.

‡In recent years the Watchtower has maintained that Russell never made a cent on the "Miracle Wheat," and that it was a contribution to the Society—"as open and above board as a Church cake sale." They characteristically omit the fact that Russell controlled the Watchtower, owning 990 of the 1,000 shares of its stock; therefore, any contributions to it were actually to him. This fact explodes nicely another Watchtower attempt to dodge the issue.

§Some Watchtower adherents deny the documentation of the above listed newspaper editions, but they are on microfilm and are available for confirmation.

Following the *Eagle's* exposing "Pastor" Russell's "Miracle Wheat" enterprise and the publication of the testimony on the basis of which Mrs. Russell obtained a separation and alimony, the "Pastor" developed the "world tour" idea. He set his printing plant to work to get out advance literature, huge bundles of which were sent to every place where he intended to appear. Then he contracted for advertising space in many American newspapers to print his imaginary sermons.

His first stop after sailing from the Pacific Coast was Honolulu. And Presto!—the newspapers in which advertising space had been engaged printed long cable dispatches which presented the "Pastor's" discourses. In one paper which printed the advertisement the opening sentences read,

"Honolulu Hawaiian Islands:

"The International Bible Students Committee of Foreign Mission Investigation stopped at Honolulu and made observations. Pastor Russell, Chairman of the Committee, delivered a public address. He had a large audience and attentive hearing."

Then follows the sermon, full of local color and allusions to the "Paradise of the Pacific":

"I can now well understand [the printed report makes the 'Pastor' say] why your beautiful island is 'The Paradise of the Pacific.' I note your wonderful climate and everything which contributes to bring about this Paradise likeness."

And so on for two columns.

It has long been known that "Pastor" Russell has a strong imagination, but now it appears that he is even capable of delivering imaginary sermons. *Pastor Russell never spoke in Honolulu during the few hours that his ship stopped there to take on coal.* In the hope of securing an accurate report of his sermon, the *Eagle* wrote to the editor of the *Hawaiian Star,* which is published in Honolulu.

The following reply was received shortly after:

In answer to your inquiry of December 19th concerning Pastor Russell, I would say that he was here for a few hours with a Bible students' committee of foreign mission investigation, but did not make a public address as was anticipated. Walter G. Smith, Editor, *Star.*

On page 18 of the same edition of the *Eagle*, February 19, 1912, photographically reproduced evidence of the "imaginary sermon" and editor Smith's letter branding it a *lie* can be found by the interested reader and leave no doubt as to "Pastor" Russell's character.

The following article, entitled "Tour of Orient branded huge advertising scheme," appeared in the January 11, 1913, *Brooklyn Daily Eagle*.

> As to the "Pastor's" methods of carrying Russellism to the heathen and the speed with which his searching investigations into the missions of the world are being conducted, the *Japan Weekly Chronicle* of January 11 supplies some interesting information. After explaining how the office of the paper had for weeks been bombarded with Russell literature and advance agents with contracts "just as if the reverend gentleman were an unregenerated theatrical company" the *Chronicle* says:
>
> "These gentlemen arrived in Japan on Saturday the 30th December. On the following day 'Pastor' Russell delivered a sermon in Tokyo entitled 'Where are the Dead?' which, though the title is a little ambiguous, does not seem to have any special connection with the mission work. On Monday it is assumed that the mission work in Japan was begun and finished, for the next day seems to have been devoted to traveling, and on Wednesday 'Pastor' Russell and his co-adjutors left Kobe for China in the same vessel in which they had arrived in Yokohama . . . the truth is that the whole expedition is merely a huge advertising scheme!"

Russell carried on many such advertising stunts; and despite his protestations about earthly governments and laws being organizations of the devil, he was always the first to claim their protection when it was convenient for him to do so.

To mention one instance in addition to the *Eagle* suit, Russell brought suit for "defamatory libel" against the Reverend J. J. Ross, pastor of the James Street Baptist Church of Hamilton, Ontario, when the minister wrote a blistering pamphlet denouncing Russell's theology and personal life. Russell lost this attempt (see *The Brooklyn Daily Eagle*, January 11, 1913) with J. F. Rutherford as his attorney. For the benefit of the interested reader, at this time, we recount the facts concerning the libel suit as it actually occurred.

In June 1912, the Reverend J. J. Ross published a pamphlet entitled, *Some Facts About the Self-Styled "Pastor" Charles T. Russell,* which minced no words in its denunciation of Russell, his qualifications as a minister, or his moral example as a pastor. Russell promptly sued Ross for "defamatory libel" in an effort to silence the minister before the pamphlet could gain wide circulation and expose his true character and the errors of his theology. Mr. Ross, however, was unimpressed by Russell's action and eagerly seized upon the opportunity as a means of exposing Russell for the fraud he was. In his pamphlet, Ross assailed Russell's teachings as revealed in *Studies in the Scriptures* as "the destructive doctrines of one man who is neither a scholar nor a theologian." Mr. Ross scathingly denounced Russell's whole system as "anti-rational, anti-scientific, anti-Biblical, anti-Christian, and a deplorable perversion of the gospel of God's Dear Son."[1]

Continuing his charges in the pamphlet, Ross exposed Russell as a pseudoscholar and philosopher who "never attended the higher schools of learning; knows comparatively nothing of philosophy, systematic or historical theology; and is totally ignorant of the dead languages."[2] It must be clearly understood that in a libel suit of the type pursued by Russell, the plaintiff (Russell) had to *prove* that the charges lodged against him by the defendant (Ross) were not true; Ross, on the other hand, had to prove that they were, or else lose the suit and stand guilty as a convicted defamer of character, while Russell's character and teachings would have been vindicated. It is significant to note in connection with these facts that Russell lost his suit against Ross when the High Court of Ontario, in session March 1913, ruled that there were no grounds for libel; and "the case was thrown out of Court by the evidence furnished by 'Pastor' Russell himself."[3]

Pastor Russell refused to give any evidence to substantiate his case, and the only evidence offered was Russell's own statements, made under oath and during cross examination by Ross's lawyer, counselor Staunton. By denying Ross's charges, Russell automatically claimed high scholastic ascendancy, recognized theological training (systematic and historical), working knowledge of the dead languages (Greek, Hebrew, etc.), and valid ordination by a recognized body.[4] To each part of Mr. Ross's pamphlet (and all was read) Russell entered vigorous denials, with the exception of the "Miracle Wheat Scandal" which he affirmed as having "a grain of truth in a sense" to it.[5] Pastor Russell had at last made a serious mistake. He had testified under oath before Jehovah God, and had sworn to tell "the truth, the whole truth, and nothing but the truth." He was soon to regret his testimony and stand in jeopardy as a perjurer, an unpleasant experience for the pastor, which more than explains his aversion to the witness chair.

In order to clarify the evidence as irrefutable, we refer any curious doubters to the files of the Watchtower Society itself, Russell vs. Ross—"defamatory libel," March 17, 1913. The authors have personally seen this transcript and compared it with the copy we had obtained. Jehovah's Witnesses cannot deny this documentary evidence; it is too well substantiated. This is no "religionist scheme" to "smear" the pastor's memory; we offer it as open proof of their founder's inherent dishonesty and lack of morals.

The following reference quotation is taken in part from Mr. Ross's pamphlet, *Some Facts and More Facts About the Self-Styled Pastor—Charles T. Russell:*

> But now what are the facts as they were brought out by the examination on March 17, 1913? As to his scholastic standing he (Russell) had sworn that what was said about it was not true. Under the examination, he admitted that at most he had attended school only seven years of his life at the public school, and that he had left school when he was about fourteen years of age.[6]

The following reproduction of the Russell vs. Ross transcript relative to the perjury charge made against Russell is taken from a copy on file in the Society's headquarters in Brooklyn.

The cross examination of Russell continued for five hours. Here is a sample of how the pastor answered.

Q: Do you know the Greek alphabet?
A: Oh yes.
Q: Can you tell me the correct letters if you see them?
A: Some of them, I might make a mistake on some of them.

Q: Would you tell me the names of those on top of the page, page 447, I have got here?

A: Well, I don't know that I would be able to.

Q: You can't tell what those letters are? look at them and see if you know.

A: My way— [He was interrupted at this point and not allowed to explain.]

Q: Are you familiar with the Greek language?

A: No.

It should be noted from this record of the testimony that Russell frequently contradicted himself, claiming first to "know" the Greek alphabet, then claiming under pressure that he might make mistakes in identifying the letters, and then finally admitting that he could not read the alphabet at all when confronted with a copy of it.

Here is conclusive evidence; the pastor, under oath, perjured himself beyond question. Can one sincerely trust the teachings of such a man who thought nothing of such evidence?

This, however, was not all of Russell's testimony, and as counselor Staunton pressed him further, the pastor admitted that he knew *nothing* about Latin and Hebrew, and neither had he ever taken a course in philosophy or systematic theology, much less attended schools of higher learning. Bear in mind now that Russell a short time before had sworn he *did* have such knowledge by denying Mr. Ross's allegations. But there was no way out now; the "pastor" was caught in a bold-faced fabrication and he knew it. However, all was not over yet. It will be remembered that Russell claimed "ordination" and equal if not superior status to ordained and accredited ministers. Staunton next smashed this illusion by demanding that Russell answer yes or no to the following questons:

Q: Is it true you were never ordained?

A: It is not true.

It was necessary at this point for Staunton to appeal to the magistrate in order to make Russell answer the question directly. The magistrate presiding ruled that Russell must answer the questions put to him. Here is the result of the cross-examination.

Q: Now, you never were ordained by a bishop, clergyman, pres-
   bytery, council, or any body of men living?
A: (*after a long pause*): I never was.

Once again, Russell's "unswerving" honesty received a rude
blow; the situation was out of his hands and Russell stood helpless as Staunton wrung statement after statement from him which
established him beyond doubt as a premeditated perjurer. The
evidence was in; the case was clear; Russell was branded a perjurer by the court's verdict, "No Bill." As a result of the court's
action, Mr. Ross's charges were proven true and the real character
of Russell was revealed, that of a man who had no scruples about
lying under oath and whose doctrines were admittedly based on
no sound educational knowledge of the subject in question.

The easily offended pastor might have practiced what he
preached for once and heeded Christ's injunction concerning the
patient enduring of reviling and persecution (Mt 5:11-12), but in
Russell's case, it is not at all applicable. Russell took every opportunity to make money, and legal clashes were frequent as a
result. He maneuvered masterfully just one jump ahead of the
law and had it not been for Rutherford, who was a clever lawyer,
the pastor might not have been so fortunate. Russell hid, whenever cornered, behind the veil of a martyr for religious toleration,
and despite the denunciation of churches and ministers, he somehow succeeded in escaping the effects of damaging publicity. The
Christian church fought him openly but without the unified effort
needed to squelch his bold approach. Some churches and pastors
were united (see *The Brooklyn Daily Eagle*, January 2, 1913,
p. 18) and called for Russell's silencing as a menace. The pastor
was also deported from Canada because he hindered mobilization
(see *The Daily Standard Union*, November 1, 1916), and in the
early stages of World War I, he was a prominent conscientious
objector as all of his followers (Jehovah's Witnesses) still are
today.

As a speaker, Russell swayed many; as a theologian, he im-
pressed no one competent; as a man, he failed before the true
God. Russell traveled extensively, spoke incessantly, and campaigned with much energy for "a great awakening" among the
people of the world. In the course of his writings and lectures,

Russell denied many of the cardinal doctrines of the Bible—the Trinity, the deity of Christ, the physical resurrection and return of Christ, eternal punishment, the reality of hell, the eternal existence of the soul, and the validity of the infinite atonement, to state a few. To be perfectly frank and honest, Russell had no training or education to justify his interpretation of Scripture. By this, it is not meant that great education is a necessary qualification for exegesis, but when a man contradicts practically every major doctrine of the Bible, he ought to have the education needed to defend (if that is possible) his arguments. Pastor Russell did not have that knowledge or even the qualifications for ordination by any recognized body. The title "Pastor" was assumed, not earned; and to document this fact, we quote from the November 1, 1916, edition of *The Brooklyn Daily Eagle*. "Although he styled himself a 'pastor' and was so addressed by thousands of followers all over the world, he had never been ordained and had no ministerial standing in any other religious sect than his own."

Psychologically, the man was an egotist whose imagination knew no bounds and who is classed (by his followers) along with Paul, Wycliffe, and Luther as a great expounder of the gospel. These are trite words for a man who proffered his writings as necessary for a clear understanding of the Scriptures and who once declared that it would be better to leave the Scriptures unread and read his books, rather than read the Scriptures and neglect his books.

For those who do not believe that the pastor made such a claim, we document the above assertion from *The Watchtower*, September 15, 1910, page 298, where the pastor makes the following statement concerning his *Studies in the Scriptures* and their "indispensable" value when examining the Bible.

> If the six volumes of "Scripture Studies" are practically the Bible, topically arranged with Bible proof texts given, we might not improperly name the volumes "The Bible in an Arranged Form." That is to say, they are not mere comments on the Bible, but *they are practically the Bible* itself. Furthermore, not only do we find that *people cannot see the divine plan in studying the Bible by itself*, but we see, also, that if anyone lays

the "Scripture Studies" aside, even after he has used them, after he has become familiar with them, after he has read them for ten years—if he then lays them aside and ignores them and goes to the Bible alone, though he has understood his Bible for ten years, our experience shows that within two years *he goes into darkness.* On the other hand, if he had merely read the "Scripture Studies" with their references and *had not read a page of the Bible as such,* he would be in the *light* at the end of two years, because he would have the light of the Scriptures.||

Nowhere was Russell's egotism or boldness better revealed than in that statement. Think of it: according to the pastor, it is impossible to understand God's plan of salvation independent of Russellite theology; and to relegate one's study to the Bible alone devoid of Russell's interpretations is to walk in darkness at the end of two years. But there is a ray of hope for all those foolish enough to study God's Word alone. If all will adopt Russellism as a guide in biblical interpretation, mankind will enter into a "new" kingdom age; for then, by virtue of the pastor's expositions, true understanding of the Bible's basic doctrines will have been arrived at. To quote Mr. Ross: "This inspiration has its origin in the pit."[7]

Jehovah's Witnesses pursue this same line of theological interpretation today. Russellism did not die with Charles Taze Russell; it lives under the new title "The Watchtower Announcing Jehovah's Kingdom." The pastor's dream has survived its author and remains today a living challenge to all Christians everywhere. Let us recognize it for what it is and unmask the unsound principles upon which it stands.

Upon Russell's death, the helm of leadership was manned by Judge Joseph Franklin Rutherford who proved himself noble in the eyes of the Society by attacking the doctrines of "organized religion" with unparalleled vigor, and whose radio talks, phonograph recordings, numerous books, and resounding blasts against Christendom reverberated down the annals of the organization until his death from cancer, on January 8, 1942, at his palatial mansion, "Beth Sarim," in San Diego, California. He was 72. Rutherford's career was no less amazing than Russell's, for the

||Emphasis added.

judge was an adversary of no mean proportions, whether in action against "organized religion," which he termed "rackets," or against those who questioned his decisions in the Society.

Throughout the years following Russell's death, Rutherford rose in power and popularity among the "Russellites," and to oppose him was tantamount to questioning the authority of Jehovah Himself. An example of this one-man sovereignty concerns the friction that occurred in the movement when Rutherford denounced Russell's pyramid prophecies scheme as an attempt to find God's will outside the Scriptures (1929). Many followers of Russell's theory left the movement as a result of this action by Rutherford, only to be witheringly blasted by the vituperative judge, who threatened that they would "suffer destruction" if they did not repent and recognize Jehovah's will as expressed through the Society.[8]

Rutherford also at times approached the inflated egotism of his predecessor, Russell, and especially when, in his textbook *Why Serve Jehovah?*, he declared, in effect, that he was the mouthpiece of Jehovah for this age and God had designated His words as the expression of divine mandate.[9] It is indeed profitable to observe that Rutherford, as do all would-be incarnations of infallibility, manifested unfathomable ignorance of God's express injunctions, especially against the preaching of "any other gospel" (Gal 1:8-9, KJV).

Fear of retaliation or rebuke was never characteristic of Judge Rutherford, and quite often he displayed complete contempt for all "religions" and their leaders. Lashing out against the persecution of the Witnesses in 1933, the tireless judge challenged the pope or any qualified representative of the Roman Catholic church to debate with him on the plight of Jehovah's Witnesses.[10] Needless to say, he was ignored. Rutherford also battled against the Federal Council of the Churches of Christ in the U.S.A. and even offered to pay half the time cost for a radio debate on the subject of persecution.[11] Once again, silence balked the vocal leader, and Rutherford abated for a time. Few things, however, were allowed to dampen the judge's vociferous thunderings, and even a term in Atlanta Federal Penitentiary in 1918 for violation of the *Espionage Act* failed to silence the judge's attacks. Rutherford was released from Atlanta in March 1919, and returned to the Witnesses fold a martyr-hero, a complex readily appropriated by all Witnesses upon the slightest pretext. Indeed, they greatly enjoy playing the role of persecuted saints. One only regrets that some of our less prudent administrators have so obligingly accommodated them.

The person of J. F. Rutherford, then, in the light of these facts, cannot be ignored by any true evaluation which seeks valid data concerning the Society's history. The great personal magnetism and the air of mystery which surround the man account most probably for his success as a leader, for he was almost a legendary figure even during his lifetime. The judge shunned photographs, although he was most photogenic and presented both an imposing and impressive figure when attired in his familiar wing collar, bow tie, and black suit. Reading glasses, which hung on a string across his honor's portly profile, accentuated the illusion of dignified importance, along with the title of judge, which, contrary to popular opinion, he did hold from the days of his early legal career, when he was a special judge of the Eighth Judicial Circuit Court of Boonville, Missouri. Rutherford also possessed a deep, powerful voice which was capable of holding large audiences with its crescendo-like effect, but he seldom appeared in public and lived a closely guarded private life. Toward the end of his life, Rutherford's reign was not overly smooth, notably when the deposed head of the Witnesses legal staff, Olin Moyle, sued Rutherford and several members of the Watchtower's board of directors in 1939 for libel and won his case, a judgment of $25,000 in 1944, two years after Rutherford's demise.

In comparing Russell and Rutherford, it must be noted that the former was a literary pygmy compared to his successor. Russell's writings were distributed, approximately fifteen or twenty million copies of them, over a period of sixty years, but Rutherford's in half that time were many times that amount. The prolific judge wrote over one hundred books and pamphlets, and his works as of 1941 had been translated into eighty languages. This, then, was the Society's second great champion, who, regardless of his many failings, was truly an unusual man by any standards. Russell and Rutherford are the two key figures in the Society's history, and without them, no doubt, the organization would never have come into existence. But conjecture never eliminated a problem, and Jehovah's Witnesses are now a problem with which every Christian must cope.

The new president of the combined organization is Nathan H. Knorr, who was elected president after Rutherford's death. Mr. Knorr is responsible for the Gilead Missionary Training School in South Lansing, New York, and has addressed 252,000 persons at the International Convention of Jehovah's Witnesses in Yankee Stadium and the Polo Grounds in New York City. Mr. Knorr is following diligently in the footsteps of Russell and Rutherford, and under his tutelage, Christianity can expect much opposition in the future.

This then is the history of Jehovah's Witnesses, the product of Charles Taze Russell, who, because he would not seek instruction in the Word of God, dedicated his unschooled talents to a lone vain search without the guidance of the Holy Spirit. This attempt has produced a cult of determined people who are persuaded in their own minds and who boldly attempt to persuade all others that the kingdom of God is "present," and that they are Jehovah's Witnesses, the only *true* servants of the living God.

The preceding material is only a fragmentary presentation of what is available in the form of vast documentary evidence, and definitely reveals beyond a shadow of reasonable doubt the faulty character of one of the greatest religious charlatans and frauds ever to masquerade as a minister of the gospel.

2

Major Doctrines and Arguments Against "Religionist" Theology

In the preparation of this data, it was important that the most precise accuracy be obtained so as not to present falsely either the history or the teachings of the Watchtower. It was in the interest of such a presentation that we submitted the following doctrinal statement to the Society for its approval. The Society returned to us our copy of these doctrines with their own corrections marked in red pencil on the sheets. Thus we are able to present for the first time in any publication of this nature, a statement of faith approved by the Watchtower Bible and Tract Society, the official spokesman for Jehovah's Witnesses. This beyond question commits them to an unretractable doctrinal statement. The doctrines which follow are therefore the self-affirmed views of the Watchtower, and we sincerely urge every honest Bible student to compare them carefully with the Holy Scriptures. Such a comparison will, we believe, more than justify their condemnation as subtle perversions by those who are "having a form of godliness but denying the power thereof" (2 Ti 3:5, KJV).

1. There is one solitary being from all eternity, Jehovah God, the Creator and Preserver of the universe and of all things visible and invisible.
2. The Word, or Logos, is "a god," a mighty god, the "beginning of the Creation" of Jehovah, and His active agent in the creation of all things. The Logos was made human as the man

Jesus and suffered death to produce the ransom or redemptive price for obedient men.

3. The Bible is the inerrant, infallible, inspired Word of God as it was originally given, and has been preserved by Him as the revealer of His purposes.

4. Satan was a great angel who rebelled against Jehovah and challenged His sovereignty. Through Satan, sin and death came upon man. His destiny is annihilation with all his followers.

5. Man was created in the image of Jehovah but willfully sinned; hence all men are born sinners and are "of the earth." Those who follow Jesus Christ faithful to the death will inherit the heavenly kingdom with Him. Men of good will who accept Jehovah and His theocratic rule will enjoy the "new earth"; all others who reject Jehovah will be annihilated.

6. The atonement is a ransom paid to Jehovah God by Christ Jesus and is applicable to all who accept it in righteousness. In brief, the death of Jesus removed the effects of Adam's sin on his offspring and laid the foundation of the new world of righteousness including the millennium of Christ's reign.

7. The man Christ Jesus was resurrected a divine spirit creature after offering the ransom for obedient man.

8. The soul of man is not eternal but mortal, and it can die. Animals likewise have souls, though man has the preeminence by special creation.

9. Hell, meaning a place of fiery torment where sinners remain after death until the resurrections, does not exist. This is a doctrine of "organized religion," not the Bible. Hell is the common grave of mankind, literally *Sheol* (Hebrew), "a place of rest in hope" where the departed sleep until the resurrection by Jehovah God.

10. Eternal punishment is a punishment, or penalty, of which there is no end. It does not mean eternal torment of living souls. Annihilation, the second death, is the lot of all those who reject Jehovah God, and it is eternal.

11. Jesus Christ returned to earth A.D. 1914, expelled Satan from heaven, and is proceeding to overthrow Satan's organization, establish the theocratic millennial kingdom, and vindicate

the name of Jehovah God. He did not return in a physical
form and is invisible as the Logos.

12. The kingdom of Jehovah is supreme, and as such cannot be
compatible with present human government (devil's visible
organization), and any allegiance to them in any way which
violates the allegiance owed to Him, is a violation of the
Scripture.

JEHOVAH'S WITNESSES' ARGUMENTS AGAINST "RELIGIONIST" DOCTRINE

The following are definitions of and arguments against what
they think the "religionists" teach.

THE TRIUNE GODHEAD AND THE DEITY OF JESUS

Definition: "The doctrine, in brief, is that there are three gods
in one: God the Father, God the Son, and God the Holy Ghost,
all three equal in power, substance and eternity."[1]

1. "The obvious conclusion therefore is that *Satan**** is the
originator of the 'trinity' doctrine."[2]
2. "The justice of God would not permit that Jesus, as a ransom,
be *more* than a perfect man; and certainly *not* be the supreme God Almighty in the flesh."[3]
3. "The truth of the matter is that the *Word* is Christ Jesus,
who did have a beginning."[4]
4. "If Jesus was God, then during Jesus' death God was dead
and in the grave."[5]
5. "If Jehovah and the dead Christ were one in substance, *the
resurrection would have been impossible*."[6]
6. "The 'trinity' doctrine was not conceived by Jesus or the
early Christians."[7]
7. "The plain truth is that this is another of *Satan's* attempts to
keep the God-fearing person from learning the truth of
Jehovah and his Son, Christ Jesus."[8]
8. "The holy spirit is the invisible active *force* of Almighty God
that moves his servants to do his will."[9]
9. "Some insist that Jesus when on earth was both God and man

****Emphasis added.

in completeness. *This theory is wrong*, however. . . . It is
also easy to be seen that Jesus *could not* be part God and
part man, because that would be more than the law re-
quired; hence divine justice could not accept such a ransom."[10]

10. "At that time (pre-incarnation) as well as subsequently, he
[Christ]† was properly known as "A god'—a mighty one . . .
As he [Christ] was the highest of all Jehovah's creation so
also he was the first, the direct creation of God, the 'only
begotten,' and then he [Christ] as Jehovah's representative,
in the exercise of Jehovah's power, and in His name, created
all things."[11]

11. "Jesus is a god, but not Jehovah."[12]

12. "There is no authority in the Word of God for the doctrine
of the Trinity of the Godhead."[13]

13. "The Holy Spirit is not a person in the Godhead, or Trinity."[14]

14. "There is no personal Holy Spirit revealed in the Scriptures."[15]

15. "The Holy Spirit is not a person, and is therefore not one of
the Gods of the Trinity."[16]

16. "Nimrod married his mother, Semiramis, so that in a sense he
was his own father, and his own son. Here was the origin
of the Trinity doctrine."[17]

THE RESURRECTION OF CHRIST AND THE ATONEMENT

1. "This firstborn one [Christ] from the dead was *not raised* out
of the grave *a human creature*, but *he was raised a spirit*."[18]

2. "He was put to death a man, but was raised from the dead
a spirit being of the highest order of the divine nature . . .
the man Jesus is dead, forever dead."[19]

3. "Whether it [the body of Jesus] was dissolved into gases or
whether it is still preserved somewhere as the grand memorial
of God's love, of Christ's obedience, and of our redemption,
no one knows."[20]

4. "So the King Christ Jesus was put to death in the flesh and
was resurrected an invisible spirit creature."[21]

5. "Our Lord's human body, the one crucified, was removed from

†Brackets added.

the tomb by the power of God . . . The Scriptures do not reveal what became of that body, except that it did not decay or corrupt."[22]

6. "The 'ransom for all' given by 'the man Christ Jesus' *does not give or guarantee everlasting life* or blessing to any man."[23]

7. "That which is redeemed is *that which was lost*, namely, perfect human life, with its rights and earthly prospects."[24]

THE RETURN OF CHRIST AND HUMAN GOVERNMENT

1. "Christ Jesus comes, not as a human, but as a glorious spirit creature."[25]

2. "Some wrongfully expect a literal fulfillment of the symbolic statements of the Bible. Such hope to see the glorified Jesus coming seated on a white cloud where every human eye will see him. . . . Since no earthly men have ever seen the Father . . . neither will they see the glorified Son."[26]

3. "It does not mean that he [Christ] is on the way, or has promised to come, but that he has already arrived."[27]

4. "Jehovah's Witnesses do not salute the flag of any nation."[28]

5. "Any national flag is a symbol or image of the sovereign power of that nation."[29]

6. "All such likenesses [symbols of a national power, eagle, sun, lion, etc.] are embraced by Exodus 20:2-6 [the commandment of idolatry]."[30]

7. "Therefore no witness of Jehovah, who ascribes salvation *only* to Him, may salute any flag of any nation without a violation of Jehovah's commandment against idolatry as stated in His Word—1 John 5:21."[31]

THE EXISTENCE OF HELL AND ETERNAL PUNISHMENT

1. "God-dishonoring religious doctrine."[32]

2. "It is so plain that the Bible hell is the tomb, the grave, that even an honest little child can understand it, but not the religious theologians."[33]

3. "And now, who is responsible for this God-dishonoring doctrine? and what is his purpose? *The promulgator of it is Satan himself;* and his purpose in introducing it has been to frighten the people away from studying the Bible and to make them hate God."[34]

4. "Imperfect man does not torture even a mad dog, but kills it; and yet the clergymen attribute to God, who is love (1 John 4:16), the *wicked crime* of torturing human creatures merely because they had the misfortune to be born sinners."[35]

5. "The doctrine of a burning hell where the wicked are tortured eternally after death cannot be true, mainly for four reasons: (1) Because it is wholly unscriptural; (2) because it is unreasonable; (3) because it is contrary to God's love; and (4) because it is repugnant to justice."[36]

The summation of the whole matter then is a clear-cut denial by Jehovah's Witnesses of both these scriptural doctrines. This great hatred of God's justice undoubtedly stems from the founder of the organization, Russell, and its chief propagandist, Rutherford, both of whom campaigned relentlessly against the eternal justice of God in the form of conscious separation and torment as revealed in God's Word. Rutherford, we believe, voiced the conviction of every true Jehovah's Witness on this vital doctrine when he said, "Eternal torture is void of the principle of love; God is love: A Creator that would torture his creatures eternally would be a *fiend* and not a God of Love."[37]

SATAN, THE DEVIL

1. "The Devil was not always the Devil. There was a time when he enjoyed a high position in God's family. He was a spirit son of God whose name was Lucifer."[38]

2. "He rebelled against the Theocratic arrangement."[39]

3. "The ultimate end of Satan is complete annihilation."[40]

4. "That which is destroyed by everlasting fire is not preserved anywhere, but is consumed for everlasting. The 'Lake of fire and brimstone' into which Satan the Devil is eventually cast means everlasting death. 'This is the second death' (Revelation 20:10)."[41]

5. "Jehovah God also says to Satan, the unfaithful 'anointed cherub that covereth': 'I will destroy thee, O covering cherub, from the midst of the stones of fire . . . thou shalt be a terror, and never shalt thou be any more' (Ezekiel 28:16-19). Satan will be dead!"[42]

MAN THE SOUL, HIS NATURE AND DESTINY

1. "Man is a combination of two things, namely, the 'dust of the ground' and 'the breath of life.' The combining of these two things (or elements) produced a living soul or creature called *man*."[43]
2. Thus we see that the claim of religionists that man has an immortal soul, and therefore differs from the beast, is not Scriptural."[44]
3. The fact that the human soul is mortal can be amply proved by a careful study of the Scriptures. An immortal soul could not die, but God's Word, at Ezekiel 18:4 says, 'Behold, all souls are mine; . . . the soul that sinneth it shall die.' "[45]
4. "It is clearly seen that even the man Christ Jesus was mortal. He did not have an immortal soul: Jesus, the human soul, died."[46]
5. "Thus it is seen that the serpent (the Devil) is the one that originated the doctrine of the inherent immortality of the soul."[47]
6. "He [man] enters into unconsciousness."[48]
7. "Thus do the Scriptures show that the natural destiny of the sinner man is death."[49]
8. But the Bible also offers a ray of hope. . . . If a man turns to God through Jesus Christ and seeks meekness and righteousness that man can gain eternal life.—Zephaniah 2:3."[50]

THE KINGDOM OF HEAVEN

1. "Who, and how many, are able to enter the Kingdom? Revelation limits the number to 144,000 that become a part of the Kingdom and stand on Mount Zion (Revelation 14:1, 3; 7:4-8)"[51]
2. "In the capacity of priests and kings of God they reign a thousand years with Christ Jesus."[52]
3. "He [Christ] went to prepare a heavenly place for his associate members, the 'body of Christ', for they too will be invisible creatures."[53]
4. "If it is to be a heavenly Kingdom, who will be the subjects of its rule? In the invisible realm angelic hosts, myriads of them, will serve as faithful messengers of the King. And on earth

the faithful men of ancient times, being resurrected, will be princes in all the earth" (Psalm 45:16; Isaiah 32:1) . . . Also the 'great multitude' of Armageddon survivors will continue to 'serve him day and night' (Revelation 7:9-17). In faithfulness these will 'multiply, and fill the earth' and their children will become obedient subjects of the Higher Powers. And finally the 'unjust' ones that are resurrected, in proving their integrity, will joyfully submit themselves to Theocratic rule. (Acts 24:15) Those who prove rebellious or who turn unfaithful during Satan's loosing at the end of Christ's thousand-year reign will be annihilated with Satan the Devil.—Revelation 20:7-15."[54]

5. "Even the Creator so loved the New World that he gave his only begotten Son to be its King (John 3:16)."[55]

6. "The undefeatable purpose of Jehovah God to establish a righteous kingdom in these last days was fulfilled A.D. 1914."[56]

7. Obey the King Christ Jesus and flee, while there is still time, to the Kingdom mountains. (Matthew 24:15-20) The time is short, for 'THE KINGDOM OF HEAVEN IS AT HAND'."[57]

Jehovah's Witnesses become intensely disturbed whenever they are referred to as "Russellites" or their theology as "Russellism." After a thorough examination of the doctrines of the Society and a lengthy comparison with the teachings of Pastor Russell, its founder, we are convinced that the two systems are basically the same, and whatever differences do exist are minute and affect in no major way the cardinal beliefs of the organization. We believe, however, that in any research project substantiating evidence should be produced for verification whenever possible. We have attempted to do this and as a result, have listed below five of the major doctrines of Jehovah's Witnesses paralleled with the teachings of Charles Taze Russell, their late pastor. We are sure that the reader will recognize the obvious relationship between the two systems, for it is inescapably evident that Russell is the author of both.

Triune Godhead

1. "This view [the Trinity] suited well the dark ages it helped to produce."[58]

2. "This . . . theory is as unscriptural as it is unreasonable."[60]

3. "If it were not for the fact that this trinitarian nonsense was drilled into us from earliest infancy and the fact that it is so soberly taught in Theological Seminaries by gray haired professors . . . nobody would give it a moment's serious consideration."[62]

4. How the great adversary [Satan] ever succeeded in fostering it [the triune Godhead] upon the Lord's peo-

1. "Does this mean that Jehovah God (Elohim) and the . . . Son are two persons but at the same time one God and members of a so called 'trinity' or 'triune god'? When religion so teaches it violates the Word of God, wrests the Scriptures to the destruction of those who are misled, and insults God-given intelligence and reason."[59]

2. "Only the religious 'trinitarians' are presumptuous enough to claim, without Scripture basis, that two other persons are equal with Jehovah God; but Jesus does not himself claim to be one of such persons."[61]

3. "The obvious conclusion, therefore, is that Satan is the originator of the 'Trinity' doctrine."[63]

ple to bewilder and mystify them and render much of the Word of God of none effect is the real mystery."[64]

The Deity of Jesus Christ

1. "Our Lord Jesus Christ is a God . . . still the united voice of the Scriptures must emphatically assert that there is but one Almighty God, the Father of all."[65]

2. "Our Redeemer existed as a spirit being before he was made flesh and dwelt amongst men. At that time, as well as subsequently, he was properly known as 'a god' a mighty one."[67]

3. "The Logos [Christ] himself was 'the beginning of the creation of God."[69]

4. "As chief of the angels and next to the Father, he

1. "The true Scriptures speak of God's Son, the Word, as 'a god.' He is a 'mighty god,' but not 'the Almighty God, who is Jehovah'—Isaiah 9:6."[66]

2. "At the time of his beginning of life he was created by the everlasting God, Jehovah, without the aid or instrumentality of any mother. In other words, he was the first and direct creation of Jehovah God . . . He was the start of God's creative work.
He was not an incarnation in flesh but was flesh, a human Son of God, a perfect man, no longer a spirit, although having a spiritual or heavenly post and background."[68]

3. "This One was not Jehovah God, but was 'existing in the form of God.' . . . He was a spirit person . . . he was a mighty one, although not almighty as Jehovah God is . . . he was a God, but not the Almighty God, who is Jehovah."[70]

4. "Being the only begotten Son of God, . . . the Word

[Christ] was known as the Archangel (highest angel or messenger), whose name, Michael signifies, 'Who as God' or 'God's Representative.' "[71]

would be a prince among all other creatures. In this office he [Christ] bore another name in heaven, which name is 'Michael' . . . Other names were given to the Son in course of time."[72]

The Resurrection of Christ

1. "Our Lord was put to death in flesh, but was made alive in spirit; he was put to death a man, but was raised from the dead a spirit being of the highest order of the divine nature."[73]

1. "In his resurrection he was no more human. He was raised as a spirit creature."[74]

2. "It could not be that the man Jesus is the second Adam, the new father of the race instead of Adam; for the Man Jesus is dead, forever dead."[75]

2. "Jehovah God raised him from the dead, not as a human Son, but as a mighty immortal spirit Son . . . So the King Christ Jesus was put to death in the flesh and was resurrected an invisible spirit creature."[76]

3. "He [Christ] instantly created and assumed such a body of flesh and such clothing as he saw fit for the purpose intended."[77]

3. "Therefore the bodies in which Jesus manifested himself to his disciples after his return to life were not the body in which he was nailed to the tree. They were merely materialized for the occasion, resembling on one or two occasions the body in which he died."[78]

4. "Our Lord's human body . . . did not decay or corrupt. . . . Whether it was dissolved into gases or whether it is still preserved somewhere . . . no one knows."[79]

4. "The firstborn one from the dead was not raised out of the grave a human creature, but he was raised a spirit."[80]

The Physical Return of Christ

1. "And in *like manner* as he went away (quietly, secretly, so far as the world was concerned, and unknown except for his followers), *so* in this manner, he comes again."[81]

2. "He comes to us in the early dawn of the Millennial Day, [Jesus] seems to say . . . Learn that I am a spirit being, no longer visible to human sight."[83]

3. "He [Christ] does not come in the body of his humiliation, a human body, which he took for the suffering of death . . . but in his glorious spiritual body."[85]

1. "Christ Jesus comes, not as a human, but as a glorious spirit creature."[82]

2. "Since no earthly men have ever seen the Father . . . neither will they see the glorified Son."[84]

3. "It is a settled Scriptural truth, therefore, that human eyes will not see him at his second coming, neither will he come in a fleshly body." . . . Christ Jesus came to the Kingdom in A.D. 1914, but unseen to men."[86]

The Existence of Hell or a Place of Conscious Torment After Death

1. "Many have imbibed the erroneous idea that God placed our race on trial for life with the alternative of *eternal torture*, whereas nothing of the kind is even hinted at in the penalty."[87]

2. "Eternal torture is nowhere suggested in the Old Testament Scriptures, and only a few statements in the New Testament can be so misconstrued as to appear to teach it."[89]

1. "The Bible hell is the tomb, the grave."[88]

2. "God-dishonoring doctrine . . . The doctrine of a burning hell where the wicked are tortured eternally after death cannot be true."[90]

In concluding this comparison, it is worthwhile to note that as far as the facts are concerned, "Jehovah's Witnesses" is simply a pseudonym for "Russellism" or "Millennial Dawnism." The similarity of the two systems is more than coincidental or accidental, regardless of the Witnesses' loud shouts to the contrary. The facts speak for themselves. Inquisitive persons may ask at this point why the organization assumed the name of "Jehovah's Witnesses." The answer is more than understandable.

After Russell's death, Judge Rutherford, the newly elected president of the Society, saw the danger of remaining Russellites, and over a period of fifteen years, he labored to cover up the pastor's unpleasant past, which did much to hinder the organization's progress. In 1931, Rutherford managed to appropriate the name "Jehovah's Witnesses," thus escaping the damaging title "Russellites." Clever man that he was, Rutherford thus managed to hide the unsavory background of Russellistic theology and delude millions of people into believing that Jehovah's Witnesses was a "different" organization. Rutherford's strategy has worked well for the Russellites, and as a result, today, those trusting souls and millions like them everywhere, sincerely believe that they are members of a "new kingdom order" under Jehovah God, when in reality, they are deluded believers in the theology of *one* man, Charles Taze Russell, who was proven to be neither a Christian nor a qualified Bible student. Jehovah's Witnesses who have not been in the movement any great period of time deny publicly and privately that they are Russellites and since few of the old-time members of Pastor Russell's personal flock are still alive, the Society in safety vehemently denounces any accusations which tend to prove that Russell's theology is the basis of the entire Watchtower system. Proof of this is found in a personal letter from the Society to the authors dated February 9, 1951, wherein, in answer to our question concerning Russell's influence, they stated—"We are not 'Russellites' for we are not following Charles T. Russell or any other imperfect man. Honest examination of our literature today would quickly reveal that it differs widely from that of Russell's, even though he was the first President of our Society."

Further than this, the Society in another letter dated November

6, 1950, and signed by Nathan H. Knorr, its legal president, declared that "the latest publications of the Watchtower Bible and Tract Society set out the doctrinal views of this organization, and I think any information you want in that regard you can find yourself without an interview." So then it is evident from these two official letters that we must judge the faith of the Jehovah's Witnesses by their literature, for they are reluctant to grant personal interviews for clarification of doctrine. However, the antipathy toward Russell's theology is not always manifested, as demonstrated when recently one of the authors was speaking with one of the head Jehovah's Witnesses teachers for the New York area and one who has been with the movement some thirty years. This zealous disciple of Russellite mythology freely admitted that the whole system as it exists today is based squarely on Pastor Russell's theology as presented in his six volumes, *Studies in the Scriptures*. Not only this, but he likewise admitted that Judge Rutherford's books also share a great place in the Society's doctrines. These facts the authors have consistently declared and are prepared to prove in comparison of extracts both from Russell's and Rutherford's writings. The Watchtower is never silent when it has ground to stand on, even if the ground is weak. However, we venture to say that they will maintain unusual silence considering the preceding evidence.

We leave the final judgment to the reader.

3

The Trinity and the Deity of Christ

ONE OF THE GREATEST DOCTRINES of the Scriptures is that of the triune Godhead (*Tes Theotetos*) or the nature of God Himself.* To say that this doctrine is a "mystery" is indeed inconclusive, and no informed minister would explain the implications of the doctrine in such abstract terms. Jehovah's Witnesses accuse "The Clergy" of doing just that, however, and it is unfortunate to note that they are, as usual, guilty of misstatement in the presentation of the facts, and even in their definition of what Christian clergymen believe the Deity to be.

Christian ministers and Christians as a whole do not believe that there are "three gods in one"[1] but *do* believe that there are three Persons all of the same substance, coequal, coexistent, and coeternal, immutable forever. There is ample ground for this belief in the Scriptures, where plurality in the Godhead is very strongly intimated if not expressly declared. Let us consider just a few of these references.

In Genesis 1:26 (KJV), Jehovah is speaking of creation, and He speaks in the plural number, "Let *us* create man in our image after *our* likeness." Now, it is obvious that God would not create man in His image and the angels' images if He were talking to them, so He must have been addressing someone else, and who, but His Son and the Holy Spirit who are equal in substance, could He address in such familiar terms? Since there is no other

---

*Jehovah's Witnesses take great delight in pointing out that the word *Trinity* does not appear as such in the Bible. They further state that since it is not a part of Scripture, it must be of pagan origin and should be discounted entirely. What the Witnesses fail to understand is that the very word *Jehovah*, which they maintain is the only true name for God, also does not appear as such in the Bible, but is an interpolation of the Hebrew consonants YHWH or JHVH, any vowels added being arbitrary. Thus it is seen that the very name by which they call themselves is just as unbiblical as they suppose the Trinity to be. (See chap. 8.) The same is true of the word *theocracy*, a favorite Jehovah's Witness term.

god but Jehovah (Is 43:10-11), not even "a lesser mighty god" as Jehovah's Witnesses affirm Christ to be, there must be a unity in plurality and substance, or the passage is not meaningful. The same is true of Genesis 11:7, at the tower of Babel, when God said, "Let us go down," and also of Isaiah 6:8, "Who will go for us" (KJV). These instances of plurality indicate something deeper than an impersonal relationship; they strongly suggest what the New Testament fully develops, namely, a tri-unity in the one God. The claim of Jehovah's Witnesses that Tertullian and Theophilus propagated and introduced the threefold unity of God into Christianity is ridiculous and hardly worth refuting. Before Tertullian or Theophilus lived, the doctrine was under study and considered sound. No one doubts that among the heathen (Babylonians and Egyptians), demon gods were worshiped, but to call the triune Godhead doctrine "of the devil"[2] as Jehovah's Witnesses do, is blasphemy and the product of untutored and darkened souls.

In the entire chapter, "Is There a Trinity?", the whole problem as to why the Trinity doctrine is "confusing" to Jehovah's Witnesses lies in their interpretation of *death* as it is used in the Bible.[3] To Jehovah's Witnesses, death is the cessation of consciousness, or *destruction*. However, no single or collective rendering of Greek or Hebrew words in any reputable lexicons or dictionary will substantiate their view. Death in the Scriptures is "separation" from the body as in the case of the first death (physical), and separation from God for eternity as in the second death (the lake of fire, Rev 20). Death never means annihilation, and Jehovah's Witnesses cannot bring in one word in the original languages to prove it does. A wealth of evidence has been amassed to prove it does not. We welcome comparisons on this point.

The rest of the chapter is taken up with childish questions. "Who ran the universe the three days Jesus was dead and in the grave?" (death again portrayed as extinction of consciousness) is a sample. "Religionists" is the label placed on all who disagree with the organization's views, regardless of the validity of the criticism. Christians do not believe that the Trinity was incarnate in Christ and that they were "three in one" during Christ's ministry. Christ voluntarily limited Himself in His earthly body, but heaven was always open to Him. At His baptism, the Holy Spirit descended like a dove, the Father spoke, and the Son was baptized. What further proof is needed to show a threefold unity? Compare the baptism of Christ (Mt 3:16-17) with the commission to preach in the threefold name of God (Mt 28:19), and the evidence is clear and undeniable. Of course, it is not possible to fathom this great revelation completely, but this we do know: there is a unity of substance, not three gods, and that unity is one in every sense, which no reasonable person can doubt after surveying the evidence. When Jesus said, "My Father is greater than I," He spoke the truth; for in the form of a servant (Phil 2:7) and as a man, the Son was subject to the Father willingly; but upon His resurrection and in the radiance of His glory (vv. 7-8), He showed forth His deity when He declared, "All authority is surrendered to me in heaven and in earth" (Mt 28:18); proof positive of His genuine nature and unity of substance. It is evident, then, that the Lord Jesus Christ was never inferior, spiritually speaking, to His Father during His sojourn on earth; and contrary to the view of Jehovah's Witnesses, even during the days of His flesh, there was no subordination of His essence, since He said that "all men should honour the Son, even as they honour the Father" (Jn 5:23, KJV).

There are many semantic problems that arise in any study of this type, and, to be sure, some difficult questions do present themselves. But the complexity of any problem does not justify its rejection or misinterpretation by persons unqualified to enter into deep exegetical study involving the original languages and their usage. Before such rash judgment as "of the devil" is applied to any doctrine, every honest effort should be made to seek out all the facts. Jehovah's Witnesses have failed to do this and as a result are properly confused.†

†First Jn 5:7 was omitted from this discussion of the Trinity, because there is some question as to its complete authenticity, although it is referred to by the three early writers, Ithacius (4th cent.), Priscillianus (A.D. 385), and Virgilius Tapsensis (5th cent.), as though genuine. *The Emphatic Diaglott* says (p. 803), "It is not cited by . . . any of the early Latin fathers . . . and was first cited (though not as it now reads)by Virgilius Tapsensis . . . in the latter end of the fifth century." This statement is contradicted by Nestle's Greek New Testament, p. 606.

Throughout the entire content of inspired Scripture, the fact of Christ's identity is clearly taught. He is revealed as Jehovah-God in human form, (Is 7:14; 9:6; Mic 5:2; Jn 1:1, 14; 8:58; 17:5; cf. Ex 3:14; and Heb 1:3; Phil 2:11; Col 2:9; and Rev 1:8, 17-18). The deity of Jesus Christ is one of the cornerstones of Christianity, and as such, has been attacked more vigorously throughout the ages than any other single doctrine of the Christian faith. Adhering to the old Arian heresy, which Athanasius, the great church Father, refuted in his famous essay "On the Incarnation of the Word," many individuals and all cults steadfastly deny the equality of Jesus Christ with God the Father, and hence the triune Deity. Jehovah's Witnesses, as has been observed, are no exception to this infamous rule. However, the testimony of the Scriptures standeth sure, and the above mentioned references alone put to silence forever this blasphemous heresy, which in the power of Satan himself deceives many with its deceitful handling of the Word of God.

The deity of Christ then is a prime answer to Jehovah's Witnesses, for if the Trinity is a reality, which it is, if Jesus and Jehovah are one and the same, then the whole framework of the cult collapses into a heap of shattered, disconnected doctrines incapable of even a semblance of congruity. We will now consider the verses in question, and their bearing on the matter.

- Isaiah 7:14, "Therefore the Lord [Jehovah] himself shall give you a sign; Behold, a virgin shall conceive, and bear a son, and shall call his name Immanuel" (KJV; lit., God, or Jehovah, with us, since Jehovah is the *only* God).
- Isaiah 9:6, "For unto us a child is born, unto us a son is given: and the government shall be upon his shoulder: and his name shall be called Wonderful, Counsellor, The mighty God, The everlasting Father, The Prince of Peace" (KJV).
- Micah 5:2, "But thou, Beth-lehem Ephratah, though thou be little among the thousands of Judah, yet out of thee shall he come forth unto me that is to be ruler in Israel; whose goings forth have been from of old, from everlasting" (KJV).

Within the realm of Old Testament Scripture, Jehovah, the Lord of hosts, has revealed His plan to appear in human form and has fulfilled the several prophecies concerning this miracle in the Person of Jesus Christ. Examination of the above listed texts will convince the student of Scripture that Jehovah has kept His promises and did become man, literally "God with us" (Mt 1:23; Lk 1:32-33; Jn 1:14).

The key to Isaiah 7:14 is the divine name "Immanuel," which can only be rightly rendered "God with us"; and since there is no other God but Jehovah, by His own declaration (Is 43:10-11), therefore Jesus Christ and Jehovah God are of the same substance in power and eternity, hence equal. This prophecy was fulfilled in Matthew 1:22-23; thus there can be no doubt that Jesus Christ is the "son of the virgin" so distinctly portrayed in Isaiah 7:14. Jehovah's Witnesses can present no argument to refute this plain declaration of Scripture, namely, that Jehovah and Christ are one and the same, since the very term *Immanuel* (God, or Jehovah, with us) belies any other interpretation.

Isaiah 9:6 in the Hebrew Bible is one of the most powerful verses in the Old Testament, in proving the deity of Christ, and incontestably declares that Jehovah Himself planned to appear in human form. The verse clearly states that all government will rest upon the "child born" and the "Son given," whose identity is revealed in the very terms used to describe His attributes. Isaiah, under the inspiration of the Holy Spirit, describes Christ as "Wonderful, Counsellor, The mighty God, The everlasting Father, The Prince of Peace" (KJV), all attributes of God alone. The term *mighty God* is in itself indicative of Jehovah, since not only is He the only God (Is 43:10-11), but the term *mighty* is applied to Him alone in relation to His deity. Jehovah's Witnesses dodge this verse by claiming that Christ is "a Mighty God,"[4] but not the almighty God (Jehovah). Since there is no article in the Hebrew text, "mighty," therefore Jehovah, is not meant. The question then arises, are there two "mighty Gods"? This we know is absurd; yet Jehovah's Witnesses persist in the fallacy, despite Isaiah 10:21 (KJV), where Isaiah (without the article) declares that "Jacob shall return" unto the "mighty God," and we know that Jehovah is by His own word to Moses "the God of Jacob" (Ex 3:6, KJV). In Jeremiah 32:18 (with the article), the prophet declares that He (Jehovah) is "the Great, the Mighty God" (two forms of saying the same thing). If we are to accept Jehovah's Witnesses' view, there must be two "Mighty Gods"; and that is impossible for there is only one true and mighty God (Is 45:22).

The prophet Micah writing in Micah 5:2, recording Jehovah's words, gives not only the birthplace of Christ (which the Jews affirmed as being the city of David, Bethlehem), but he gives a clue as to His identity—namely God in human form. The term *goings forth* can be rendered "origin,"[5] and we know that the only one who fits this description, whose origin is "from everlasting" must be God Himself, since He alone is "the eternally existing One" (Is 44:6, 8 cf. Ex 3:14). The overwhelming testimony of these verses alone ascertains beyond reasonable doubt the deity of the Lord Jesus Christ, who became man, identified Himself with us in that incarnation, and offered Himself "once for all" a ransom for many, the eternal sacrifice who is able to save to the uttermost whoever will appropriate His cleansing power.

- John 1:1, "In the beginning [or origin, Greek, *arche*] was the Word [*Logos*] and the Word was with God [*Ton Theon*] and the Word was God [*Theos*]" (KJV).

Contrary to the translations of *The Emphatic Diaglott* and the *New World Translation,* the Greek grammatical construction leaves no doubt whatsoever that this is the only possible rendering of the text. The subject of the sentence is *Word* (*Logos*), the verb, *was*. There can be no direct object following *was*, since according to grammatical usage, intransitive verbs take no objects but take instead predicate nominatives which refer back to the subject, in this case, *Word* (Logos).‡ It is therefore easy to see that no article is needed for *Theos* (God), and to translate it "a god" is both incorrect grammar and poor Greek, since *Theos* is the predicative nominative of *was* in the third sentence-clause of the verse and must refer back to the subject, *Word* (*Logos*). Christ, then, if He is the Word "made flesh" (Jn 1:14, KJV) can be no one else except God, unless the Greek text and consequently God's Word be denied.

Jehovah's Witnesses, in their *New World Translation,* attempt

‡Colwell's rule clearly states that a definite predicate nominative (*Theos*—God) *never* takes an article when it precedes the verb (*was*) as in John 1:1.

to discredit the Greek text on this point, for they realize that if Jesus and Jehovah are one in nature, their theology cannot stand, since they deny that unity of nature.[6] The refutation of their arguments on this point is conclusive.

The claim is that since the definite article is used with *Theon* and not with *Theos* in John 1:1, therefore the omission is designed to show a difference; the alleged difference being that in the first case, the one true God (Jehovah) is meant, while in the second, "a god," other than, and inferior to, the first is meant, this latter "god" being Jesus Christ.

The *New World Translation* claims that the rendering "a god" is correct because "all the doctrine of sacred Scriptures bears out the correctness of this rendering."[7] This remark focuses attention on the fact that the whole problem involved goes far beyond this text. Scripture does in fact teach the full and equal deity of Christ. Why then is so much made of this one verse? It is probably because of the surprise effect derived from the show of pseudoscholarship in the use of a familiar text. Omission of the article with *Theos* does not mean that "a god" other than the one true God is meant. Let one examine these passages where the article is not used with *Theos* and see if the rendering "a god" makes sense (Mt 5:9; 6:24; Lk 1:35, 78; 2:40; Jn 1:6, 12, 13, 18; 3:2, 21; 9:16, 33; Ro 1:7, 17, 18; 1 Co 1:30; 15:10; Phil 2:11, 13; Titus 1:1). The "a god" contention proves too weak and is inconsistent. To be consistent in this rendering of "a god," Jehovah's Witnesses would have to translate every instance where the article is absent as "a god (nominative), of a god (genitive), to or for a god (dative)." This they do not do in Matthew 5:9; 6:24; Luke 1:35, 78; John 1:6, 12, 13, 18; Romans 1:7, 17. (See *New World Translation* and *Emphatic Diaglott* at above mentioned references.)

You cannot honestly render *Theos* "a god" in John 1:1, and then *Theou* "of God" (Jehovah), in Matthew 5:9, Luke 1:35, 78; and John 1:6, when *Theou* is the genitive case of the *same* noun (second declension), *without* an article and *must* be rendered (following Jehovah's Witnesses' argument) "of *a* god" not "of God" as both the *Emphatic Diaglott* and *New World Translation* put it. We could list at great length, but suggest consultation of the Greek New Testament by either D. Erwin Nestle or Westcott and Hort, in conjunction with *The Elements of Greek* by Francis Kingsley Ball, on noun endings. So then, if Jehovah's Witnesses must persist in this fallacious "a god" rendition, they can at least be consistent, which *they are not,* and render every instance where the article is absent in the same manner. The truth of the matter is that Jehovah's Witnesses use and remove the articular emphasis whenever and *wherever* it suits their fancy regardless of grammatical laws to the contrary. In a translation as important as God's Word, every law must be observed. Jehovah's Witnesses have not been consistent in their observance of those laws.

The writers of the note have also exhibited another trait common to Jehovah's Witnesses, that of half quoting or misquoting a recognized authority to bolster their ungrammatical renditions. On page 776 (NWT)§, when quoting Dr. Robertson's words, "Among the ancient writers O THEOS was used of the god of the absolute religion in distinction from the mythological gods," they fail to note that in the second sentence following, Dr. Robertson says, "In the New Testament, however, while we have PROS TON THEON (John 1:1, 2) it is far more common to find *simply THEOS,* especially in the Epistles."||

In other words, the writers of the New Testament frequently do not use the article with *Theos* and yet the meaning is perfectly clear in the context, namely that the one true God is intended. Let one examine the following references where in successive verses and even in the same sentence the article is used with *one* occurrence of *Theos* and *not* with another form, and it will be absolutely clear that no such drastic inferences can be drawn from John's usage in John 1:1-2. (Mt 4:3-4; 12:28; Lk 20:37-38; Jn 3:2; 13:3; Ac 5:29-30; Ro 1:7-8, 17-19; 2:16-17; 3:5, 22-23; 4:2-3.)

The doctrine of the article is important in Greek; it is *not* used indiscriminately. But we are *not* qualified to be sure in *all* cases what is intended. Dr. Robertson is careful to note that "it is only of recent years that a really scientific study of the article has been made."[8] The facts are not all known, and no such drastic

§*New World Translation.* All quotes are from the 1950 edition.
||Emphasis added.

conclusion as the writers of the appendix note draw should be dogmatically affirmed.

It is nonsense to say that a simple noun can be rendered "divine," and that an anarthrous noun conveys merely the idea of quality (NWT, pp. 773-74). The authors of this note themselves later render the same noun *Theos* as "a god" not as "a quality." This is a self-contradiction in the context.

In conclusion, the position of the writers of this note is made clear (NWT, p. 774); according to them, it is "unreasonable" that the Word (Christ) should be the God with whom He was (Jn 1:1). Their own manifestly erring reason is made the criterion for determining scriptural truth. One need only note the obvious misuse in their quotation from Dana and Mantey (pp. 774-75). Mantey clearly means that the "Word was Deity" in accord with the overwhelming testimony of Scripture, but the writers have dragged in the interpretation "a god" to suit their own purpose, which purpose is the denial of Christ's deity, and as a result a denial of the Word of God. #

Since the publication of Jehovah's Witnesses Kingdom interlinear translation of the Greek Scriptures in 1969, the Watchtower has quite literally backed itself into a corner with its translation of John 1:1 as it appears in the *New World Translation*. In their *New Kingdom Interlinear Translation* of John 1:1, they render the Greek text on the left side of the page: "In the beginning was the Word, and the Word was toward the God and god was the Word." Directly across the page in the right column, the *New World Translation* says, "In beginning the Word was, and the Word was with God and the Word was *a* god." It appears that the Watchtower is apparently trying to have its cake and eat it too. The Word (Christ who became flesh, see v. 14) is called God on one side of the page and *a* god on the other. Evidence of genuine grammatical confusion, and God, the Scripture reminds us, is not the author of confusion!

It is unnecessary to pursue this point any further, except to note that in their translation, "god was the Word," *God* is spelled with

#Dr. Mantey has formally repudiated the out-of-context quoting and general misrepresentation of his views in a private letter recently made public, and accuses the Watchtower of gross error in their handling of his grammar. See Appendix.

a small *g*, another subtle attempt to demote Christ to the rank of demigod, apparently oblivious to the fact that the existing manuscripts of the New Testament were all written in capital letters, and the Witnesses have always made a great point of emphasizing capitals in John 1:1, when it came to translating the Greek *Theos*. There is no grammatical reason for failing to capitalize *God* here; in fact, according to Colwell's rule, it must be.

• John 8:58, "Jesus said unto them . . . Before Abraham was [born], I am" (KJV).

In comparing this with the Septuagint translation of Exodus 3:14 and Isaiah 43:10-13, we find that the translation is identical. In Exodus 3:14, Jehovah, speaking to Moses, said, "I AM," which is synonymous with God. Jesus literally said to them, "I AM Jehovah" (I AM), and it is clear that they understood Him to mean just that; for they attempted, as the next verse reveals, to stone Him. Hebrew law on this point states five cases in which stoning was legal, and bear in mind that the Jews were legalists. Those cases were: (1) Having a familiar spirit, Leviticus 20:27; (2) Cursing (blasphemy), Leviticus 24:10-23; (3) False prophets who lead to idolatry, Deuteronomy 13:5-10; (4) Stubborn son, Deuteronomy 21:18-21; and (5) Adultery and rape, Deuteronomy 22:21-24 and Leviticus 20:10. Now, the only legal ground the Jews had for stoning Christ (and actually they had none at all) was the second violation, namely, blasphemy. Many zealous Jehovah's Witnesses maintain that the Jews were going to stone Him because He called them children of the devil (Jn 8:44). But if this were true, why did they not stone Him on other occasions (Mt 12:34; 23:33) when He called them sons of vipers? The answer is simple. They could not stone Christ on that ground because they were bound by the law which gives only five cases, and would have condemned them on their own grounds had they used "insult" as a basis for stoning. This is not all, however, for in John 10:33, the Jews again attempted to stone Christ and accused Him of making Himself God (not *a god*, which subject has already been treated at length).** Let us be logical then;

** Jehovah's Witnesses point to the *New English Bible's* rendering of this as "a god" as proof of the validity of their translation. The fact is, however, that the NEB mistranslated this passage originally. However, in the 1971 edition, the NEB modified the translation to "blasphemy," omitting both *a god* or *God*.

if the Jews observed the laws of stoning on other occasions when they might better have been insulted, why would they violate the law as they would have had to do if Jehovah's Witnesses are right in John 8:58? Little more need be said. The argument is ridiculous in its context; there is only *one* "I AM" in the Scriptures (Is 44:6; 48:12; Rev 1:8 and 17), and Jesus laid claim to that identity for which the Jews, misinterpreting the law, set about to stone Him.

Jehovah's Witnesses declare that the Greek rendering of *Ego Eimi* (I AM) in John 8:58 is "properly rendered in the 'perfect indefinite tense' (I have been), not 'I am'."[9] To unmask this bold perversion of the Greek text, we shall now examine it grammatically to see if it has any valid grounds for being so translated.

It is difficult to know what the author of the note on page 312 (NWT) means, since he *does not* use standard grammatical terminology, nor is his argument documented from standard grammars. The aorist *infinitive*, as such, *does not* form a clause. It is the adverb *prin* which is significant here, so that the construction should be called *prin* clause. The term *perfect indefinite* is an invention of the author of the note, so it is impossible to know what is meant. The real problem in the verse is the verb *Ego Eimi*. Dr. Robertson, who is quoted as authoritative by the NWT (p. 775), states that *eimi* is "absolute."[10] This means there is *no* predicate expressed with it. This usage occurs four times (Jn 8:24, 58; 13:19; 18:5). In these places, the term is the same used by the Septuagint at Deuteronomy 32:39; Isaiah 43:10; and 46:4, to render the Hebrew phrase "I (am) He." The phrase occurs *only* where Jehovah's Lordship is reiterated. The phrase then is a claim to full and equal deity. The incorrect and rude rendering of the NWT only serves to illustrate the difficulty of evading the meaning of the phrase and the context.

The meaning of the phrase in the sense of full deity is especially clear at John 13:19, where Jesus says that He has told them things before they came to pass, that when they do come to pass the disciples may believe that *Ego Eimi* (I AM). Jehovah is the only one who knows the future as a present fact. Jesus is telling them beforehand that when it does come to pass in the future, they may know that "I AM" (*Ego Eimi*), that *He is Jehovah!*

In conclusion, the facts are self-evident and undeniably clear: the Greek allows no such impositions as "I have been."†† The term is translated correctly "I AM," and since Jehovah is the only "I AM" (Ex 3:14; Is 44:6), He and Christ are one in nature, power, and eternity, truly the fullness of the "Deity" in the flesh.

> Hebrews 1:3, "He [Christ] is the reflection of His [Jehovah's] glory, and the image imprinted by his [Jehovah's] Substance, and He [Christ] sustains all things by the word of His power" (NWT).

This passage of Scripture, we believe, clarifies beyond doubt the deity of Jesus Christ. It would be illogical and unreasonable to suppose that Christ who is the image imprinted by Jehovah's *substance* is not *of* the substance of Jehovah and hence God, or the second Person of the triune Deity. No creation is ever declared to be of God's very "substance," or "essence" (*upostaseos*, Greek); therefore the eternal Word, who is "the fulness of the Godhead [Deity] bodily" (Col 2:9, KJV), cannot be a creation, or a created being. The writer of the book of Hebrews clearly intended to portray Christ as Jehovah, or he never would have used such explicit language as "the image imprinted by His substance," and as Isaiah 7:14 clearly states, the Messiah was to be Immanuel, literally, "God with us." Jehovah's Witnesses attempt the articular fallacy of "a god" instead of God, in reference to Immanuel; but if there has been "no god formed before or after me" (Jehovah speaking in Is 43:10, KJV), then it is impossible on that ground alone, namely, God's declaration, for any other god ("a god" included) to exist. Their argument, based on a grammatical abstraction, fails to stand here; and the deity of the Lord Jesus, as always, remains unscathed.

> Hebrews 13:8, "Jesus Christ the same yesterday and today, and forever" (NWT).

This is indeed a wonderful testimonial to God the Son who never changes and remains the same eternally. The literal trans-

††The Watchtower's contention on this point is that the phrase in question is an "historical present" used in reference to Abraham, hence permissible. This is a classic example of Watchtower double-talk. Jesus was not narrating but arguing, and the "historical present" is used in narrative not argument, as any standard grammar reveals.

lation of Hebrews 13:8 reads, "Jesus Christ the same yesterday, today and into the everlasting," which gives added proof to His everlasting heritage and coexistence with the Father.

But let us bear in mind that Jehovah's Witnesses reject the doctrine of the triune Deity and condemn it as "of the devil" so the deity of Christ is not accepted by them. However, unknowingly, they have affirmed it beyond doubt, for in the NWT (p. 661, marg.), they refer the reader to Revelation 1:17 in cross reference to Hebrews 13:8 and irrevocably declare that the Christ of Hebrews 13:8 is the "First and the Last" of Revelation 1:17. If Christ is the First and the Last in Revelation 1:17, He has to be the Alpha and Omega of Revelation 1:8 and by their *own* rendition, 1:8 reveals "Jehovah God" (NWT). Either there are two Firsts and Lasts, which is impossible since Jehovah affirms that He alone is the First and the Last (Is 48:12), or they are identical, and this we know to be true for Jesus claimed to be the "I AM" (Jn 8:58). (Cf. Is 51:12; 52:6; for further proof.)

> Phil 2:11, "And *that* every tongue should confess that Jesus Christ is Lord, to the glory of God the Father" (KJV).

If we compare this verse of Scripture with Colossians 2:9 and Isaiah 45:23, we cannot help but see the full deity of the Lord Jesus in its true light.

Jehovah spoke in Isaiah 45:23 and said, "I have sworn by myself, the word is gone out of my mouth in righteousness, and shall not return. That unto me every knee shall bow, every tongue shall swear" (KJV). In Colossians 2:9, the apostle Paul, writing under the inspiration of the Holy Spirit, declares, "For in him [Christ] dwelleth all the fulness of the Godhead bodily" (KJV). The literal translation of the Greek word *theotetos* (Godhead) is "deity," so in Christ all the fullness (*pleroma*) of the Deity resides in the flesh (*somatikos*).

In Thayer's *Greek-English Lexicon of the New Testament*, which is referred to as being "comprehensive" (NWT, p. 19), a complete analysis of *theotetos* (Godhead, deity) is given, especially its interpretation in the context of Colossians 2:9. Jehovah's Witnesses will do well to remember that Thayer was a Unitarian (one who denies the deity of Christ) and therefore more prone to accept their interpretations than those of evangelical Christianity. But despite his theological views, Thayer was a Greek scholar whose integrity in the presentation of facts, despite their disagreement with his beliefs, is the trait exemplified in all good critics and honest scholars. On page 288 of the edition of 1886, Thayer states that *Theotetos* [Godhead, Deity] is a form of *Theot* [Deity] or in his own words "i.e., the state of Being God, Godhead" (Col 2:9)![11] In other words, Christ was the fullness of "The Deity" (Jehovah) in the flesh! *The Emphatic Diaglott* correctly translates *Theotetos* "Deity"; but the NWT erroneously renders it "the divine quality," which robs Christ of His deity. Jehovah's Witnesses arrive at this inaccurate translation by substituting the word *Theiotes*, a form of *Theiot* (divinity) and thus escaping the condemning evidence of "The Deity" (Jehovah) *Tes Theotetos*. However, documentary evidence reveals that they cannot rightfully do this for in Thayer's own words, "THEOT (Deity) *differs* from THEIOT (divinity) as essence differs from quality or attribute."[12] This fact again exposes the deception employed by the Watchtower to lead the unwary Bible student astray into the paths of blasphemy against the Lord Jesus. It is improper, it *cannot be* so translated, the substitution of one word for another in translation is pure scholastic dishonesty, and Jehovah's Witnesses can produce no authority for this bold mistranslation of the Greek text. Jesus Christ, according to the words themselves, is the same "essence" and "substance" as Jehovah, and as the essence (deity) differs from the *quality* (divinity) so He is God— *Tes Theotetos* (The Deity)—Jehovah manifest in the flesh.

That Jesus and Jehovah are one in nature dare not be questioned from these verses which so clearly reveal the plan and purpose of God. Paul sustains this argument in his epistle to the Philippians when he ascribes to the Lord Jesus the identity of Jehovah as revealed in Isaiah 45:23. Paul proclaims boldly, "That at the name of Jesus every knee should bow . . . and that every tongue should confess that Jesus Christ is Lord to the glory of God the Father" (Phil 2:11, KJV). It is a well-known biblical fact that the highest glory one can give to God is to acknowledge and worship Him in the Person of His Son, and as Jesus Himself said, "No man cometh unto the Father, but by *me*" (Jn 14:6, KJV) and "all men should honour the Son, even as they honour the Father" (Jn 5:23, KJV).

It is therefore clear from the context that the wonder of the Godhead is specifically revealed in Jesus Christ to the fullest extent, and it is expedient for all men to realize the consequences to be met if any refuse the injunctions of God's Word and openly deny the deity of His Son who is "the true God, and eternal life" (1 Jn 5:20, KJV).

> Rev 1:8, "I am Alpha and Omega [Greek—First and Last— A to Z] says JEHOVAH GOD, the One who is and who was and who is coming, the Almighty" (NWT).

In the seventh, eighth, seventeenth, and eighteenth verses of the first chapter of Revelation, a unique and wonderful truth is again affirmed, namely, that Jesus Christ and Jehovah God are of the same "substance," hence coequal, coexistent and coeternal, in short, one nature in its fullest sense. We shall pursue that line of thought at length in substantiating this doctrine of Scripture.

Comparing Matthew 24:30 with Revelation 1:7, it is inescapably evident that Jesus Christ is the "One coming with clouds" in both the references mentioned.

> And then shall appear the sign of the Son of man in heaven: and then shall all the tribes of the earth mourn, and they shall see the Son of man coming in the clouds of heaven with power and great glory (Mt 24:30, KJV).
>
> Behold, he cometh with clouds; and every eye shall see him, and they also which pierced him: and all kindreds of the earth shall wail because of him. Even so, Amen (Rev 1:7, KJV).

Following this train of thought, we find that Jehovah declares, in Isaiah 44:6, that He alone is the First and the Last and the *only* God, which eliminates forever any confusion as to there being two Firsts and Lasts. Since Jehovah is the only God, then how can the *Logos* be "a god," a lesser god than Jehovah, as Jehovah's Witnesses declare in John 1:1? (*Emphatic Diaglott* and NWT). Many times Jehovah declares His existence as the "only" God and Saviour (Is 41:4; 43:11-13; 44:6; 45:5; 48:12). This is indeed irrefutable proof, since Christ could not be our Saviour or Redeemer if He were not Jehovah, for Jehovah is the only Saviour

(Is 43:11). However, despite the testimony of Scripture that "before me there was no God formed, neither shall there be after me" (Is 43:10, KJV), the "a god" fallacy is pursued and taught by Jehovah's Witnesses in direct contradiction to God's Word.‡‡

Revelation 1:17-18 and 2:8 add further weight to the deity of Christ, for they reveal Him as the First and the Last who became dead and lives forever. Now since Jehovah is the only First and Last (cf. Isaiah references), either He and Christ are one, or to claim otherwise, Jehovah's Witnesses must deny the authority of Scripture.

It is imperative to the argument, relative to the usage of Alpha and Omega, that other passages using the same terms be analyzed within their respective contexts in the book of Revelation. One need only turn to Revelation 21 and 22 to see how John, under the inspiration of the Holy Spirit, developed this theme.

"And he said unto me, It is done. I am Alpha and Omega, the beginning and the end. I will give unto him that is athirst of the fountain of the water of life freely. He that overcometh shall inherit all things; and I will be his God, and he shall be my son" (Rev 21:6-7, KJV).

It is apparent from the context of this passage, that John hears the voice of God (21:3). Verse 5 indicates that it is God sitting upon the throne who declares that He will make all things new. The Alpha and the Omega of Revelation in chapter 21 is Jehovah God. Turning to Revelation chapter 22, there are three repetitions of a specific phrase: verse 7, "Behold I come quickly"; verse 12, "Behold, I come quickly; and my reward is with me"; and verse 20, "Amen. Even so, come, Lord Jesus" (KJV). It is quite enlightening to learn from this context that the same person who says, "I come quickly" also says, "I am Alpha and Omega, the beginning and the end, the first and the last." He further identifies Himself in verse 16, "I Jesus have sent mine angel to testify unto you these things in the churches. I am the root and the offspring of David, and the bright and morning star" (KJV). *Alpha* and *Omega* in Greek as we have seen quite literally means "first and last," but here, God expands it, beginning and end, first and

‡‡See 1 Co 8:4-6, where Paul points out that an idol is nothing and, even though men worship things (idols, position, material possessions, etc.) as gods, there is only one true and living God. Cf. Deu 6:4; 1 Ti 2:5.

last, and when these passages are coupled with Revelation 1, 7, and 8, and Revelation 1:16-18, Jesus Christ emerges as possessing the identity of Jehovah God. (See also Is 44:6, 8 and 45:22, where Jehovah identifies Himself as First and Last.)

The Watchtower Society weakly attempts to explain all of this away by pointing out that in Revelation 1:1, Jehovah gave the Revelation to Jesus Christ; therefore, it is Jesus Christ speaking *as* Jehovah, or in Jehovah's place. This disintegrates immediately in the light of Revelation 1:17*b* and 18, "Fear not; I am the first and the last: I am he that liveth, and was dead; and, behold, I am alive for evermore, Amen; and have the keys of hell and of death" (KJV).

If Jesus is here speaking for Jehovah God, the Father, then the Father died and came to life again, a direct contradiction of the biblical record, where it is evident that the Son died, not the Father; so the argument that Jesus is only speaking as Jehovah falls by its own weight.

In order to be consistent, we must answer the arguments advanced by Jehovah's Witnesses concerning the use of *First* and *Last* (*protos*, Greek) in Revelation 1:17 and 2:8.

By suggesting the translation of *prototokos* (first born) instead of *protos* (first) in these passages (see footnotes in NWT and *Emphatic Diaglott*), Jehovah's Witnesses attempt to rob Christ of His deity and make Him a created being with "a beginning."[13] When approached on this point, they quickly refer you to Colossians 1:15 and Revelation 3:14, "proving" that the Logos had "a beginning" (see Jn 1:1, *Emphatic Diaglott* and NWT). To any informed Bible student, this argument is fallacious. J. H. Thayer's Greek-English lexicon, which is quoted as authoritative and reliable (NWT, p. 19), states that the only correct rendering of *protos* is "First," and, in Thayer's own words, "THE ETERNAL ONE" [Jehovah] (Rev 1:17). Here again, the deity of Christ is vindicated.

Further proof of this synthesis is the fact that the best and most authoritative manuscripts (Sinaiticus, Vaticanus) have *protos* "First." The Alexandrinian manuscript, since it possesses no accent marks, should be translated "Original Bringer Forth"§§

§§Or more literally, "First Begetter." See Heb 1:2.

(Erasmus), in keeping with the laws of textual criticism (Col 1:15). In short, the whole problem is one of accentuation. Since there are no marks of punctuation or accent in the Alexandrinian manuscript wording of Revelation 1:17 and 2:8, and since all the other manuscripts have *protos* "First," it is a contradiction to accentuate *prototokos* so as to make Christ a created being instead of the Creator. The correct accentuation of *prototokos* agrees with all the other manuscripts in portraying Christ as "The original bringer forth," which is as it should be. These truths, coupled with the fact that all reliable translations and translators bear out the rendering "First" in preference to "First Born," expose this attempt to pervert the Word of God.

Jesus said, "I am Alpha and Omega, the beginning and the end, the first and the last" (Rev 22:13, KJV), and not only this, but it is He who is revealing the mysteries to John (Rev 1:1 and 22:16) and declaring Himself to be the "faithful witness" (Rev 1:5, KJV) who testifies "I come quickly" (Rev 22:20, KJV). It is evident then that Jesus is the one testifying and the one coming (Rev 1:2, 7) throughout the book of Revelation, since it is by His command (Rev 22:16) that John records everything. So in honesty, we must acknowledge His Sovereignty as the "First and Last" (Is 48:12 and Rev 1:17), the Lord of all and the eternal Word of God incarnate (Jn 1:1, 14).

Revelation 3:14 asserts that Christ is the "beginning of the creation of God" and Colossians 1:15 (KJV) states that Christ is "the firstborn of every creature." These verses in no sense indicate that Christ was a created being except in the physical sense (Jn 1:14) at His incarnation (Lk 1:35). The Greek word *arche* (Rev 3:14) can be correctly rendered "origin" and is so translated in John 1:1 of Jehovah's Witnesses' own New World Translation. Revelation 3:14, then, declares that Christ is the faithful and true witness, the "origin" || || of the creation of God. This corroborates Hebrews 1:2 and Colossians 1:16-17 in establishing Christ as the Creator of all things and, hence, God (Gen 1:1). Christ is the Firstborn of all creation since He is the new Creation, conceived without sin (Lk 1:35), the last Adam (1 Co 15:45, 47) who is

---

|| ||Or "source." See Bishop Ronald Knox's *Translation of the Bible* (Roman Catholic), also Edgar J. Goodspeed,-*The New Testament, An American Translation,* Reprint (Chicago: U. of Chicago, 1923).

the fulfillment of the divine promise of the God-man (Is 7:14; 9:6; Mic 5:2) and the Redeemer of the world (Col 1:14). John 3:13 states that no one has ascended into heaven but Christ who came down; Philippians 2:11 declares that He is Lord (*Kurios*, Greek), and *not* a created being or "a god."

The Lord Jesus is also the Firstborn of the dead (Rev 1:5); that is, the first one to rise in a glorified body (*not* a spirit form; see Lk 24:39-40), which type of body Christians will someday possess as in the words of the apostle John, "It doth not yet appear what we shall be: but we know that, when he shall appear, we shall be like [similar to] him, for we shall see him as he is" (1 Jn 3:2, KJV). We know that these promises are sure for He is faithful who promised (Heb 10:23) and all who deny the deity of Christ might well take cognizance of His warning and injunction when the Spirit said,

> For I testify unto every man that heareth the words of the prophecy of this book, If any man shall add unto these things, God shall add unto him the plagues that are written in this book: And if any man shall take away from the words of the book of this prophecy, God shall take away his part out of the book of life, and out of the holy city, and from the things which are written in this book" (Rev 22:18-19, KJV).

- John 17:5: "And now, O Father, glorify thou me with thine own self with the glory which I had with thee before the world was" (KJV).

This passage of Scripture in cross reference with Isaiah 42:8 and 48:11 proves conclusively the identity of the Lord Jesus, and is a fitting testimony to the deity of Christ.

In Isaiah 42:8, Jehovah Himself is speaking, and He emphatically declares, "I am the LORD: that is my name: and my glory will I not give to another, neither my praise to graven images" (KJV). Again in Isaiah 48:11, Jehovah is speaking and He declares "For mine own sake, even for mine own sake, will I do it: for how should my name be polluted? and I will not give my glory unto another" (KJV).

In these two references in Isaiah, Jehovah irrevocably declares that His divinely inherent glory, which is of His own nature, cannot and will not be given to any person other than Himself. There is *no* argument Jehovah's Witnesses can erect to combat the truth of God as revealed in these passages of Scripture. The inherent glory of God belongs to God alone, and by His own mouth, He has so ordained it to be. # #

The Lord Jesus Christ, when He prayed in John 17:5, likewise irrevocably revealed that He would be glorified with *the glory of the Father* and that the glory of the Father (Jehovah) was not new to Him, since He affirmed that He possessed it, *with* (*para*, Greek) the Father ("the glory which I had with thee") even before the world came into existence. Jehovah's Witnesses attempt to answer this by saying that if He were God, where was His glory while He walked the earth?

In answer to this question, the Scriptures list at least four separate instances where Christ manifested His glory and revealed His power and deity. On the mount of transfiguration (Mt 17:2), Christ shone with the inherent glory of God, which glory continued undiminished when, in John 18:6, the Lord applied to Himself the "I AM" of Jehovahistic identity that radiated glory enough to render His captors powerless at His will. John 17:22 also confirms the manifestation of Jehovah's glory, when Jesus, looking forward to the cross, prays for His disciples and affirms the origin of His glory as being the substance of God. The resurrection glory of Christ also serves to illustrate His deity and reveal it as of God Himself.

So, the argument Jehovah's Witnesses advance, to the effect that Christ did not manifest the glory of Himself, is invalid and finds no basis in the Scriptures. The truth of the whole matter is that the Lord Jesus did reveal the true glory of His nature in the very works He performed, and as John says (1:14, KJV): "We beheld his glory . . . full of grace and truth."

St. Paul, in the second chapter of Philippians, removes all doubt

#God, however, bestowed upon the incarnate Word a certain glory manifested in the presence of the Holy Spirit through whose power and agency Christ worked while in the flesh and Jesus in turn bestowed this upon His followers (Jn 17:22), but it was *not* the glory of God's nature but instead the abiding presence of His Spirit and the two should not be confused. Jesus prayed to receive *back* again the glory He had with the Father "before the world was" (17:5), and it was *not* the glory given to Him as the Messiah, which glory Christ promised to share with His disciples (v. 22). Nowhere are the two equated.

on this question when guided by the Holy Spirit, he writes that Christ never ceased to be Jehovah even during His earthly incarnation. It is interesting to note that the Greek term *uparchon*, translated "being" in Philippians 2:6, literally means "remaining or not ceasing to be," hence in the context Christ never ceased to be God, and "remained" in His basic nature; He was truly "God manifest in the flesh."

A Jehovah's Witness interviewed recently, in attempting to escape the obvious declaration of Christ's deity as revealed in this text, asserted that the word *with* (*para*, Greek) in John 17:5, really means "through," and therefore the glory that is spoken of is not proof of Christ's deity, since the glory is Jehovah's and is merely shining "through" the Son; it is not His own but a manifestation of Jehovah's glory.

Once again, we are confronted with the problem of illogical exegesis, the answer to which must be found in the Greek text itself. We must believe that the grammar of the Bible is inspired by God if we believe that God inspired the writers, or how else could He have conveyed His thoughts without error? Would God commit His inspired words to the failing grammatical powers of man to record? He could not do this without risking corruption of His message; therefore, as the wise and prudent Lord that He is, He most certainly inspired the grammar of His servants that their words might transmit His thoughts without error, immutable and wholly dependable. With this thought in mind, let us consider the wording and construction of the verse.

The Greek word *para* (with) is used in the dative case in John 17:5 and is not translated "through" (*dia*, Greek), but is correctly rendered, according to Thayer's lexicon, as "with," and Thayer quotes John 17:5, the very verse in question, as his example of how *para* (with) should be translated.

Never let it be said that *para* in this context indicates anything less than possessive equality—"the glory which I had *with* thee before the world was." The Lord Jesus Christ clearly meant that He as God the Son was the possessor of divine glory along with the Father and the Holy Spirit before the world was even formed. Christ also declared that He intended to appropriate that glory in all its divine power once again, pending the resurrection of

His earthly temple, which by necessity, since it was finite, voluntarily veiled His eternal power and deity (Phil 2:5-8). The glory He spoke of did not only shine through the Father; it was eternally inherent in the Son, and since John, led by the Holy Spirit, deliberately chose *para* (with) in preference to *dia* (through), the argument that Jehovah's Witnesses advance cannot stand up. The Lord Jesus claimed the same glory of the Father as His own, and since Jehovah has said that He will not give His inherent glory to another (Is 42:8), the unity of substance between Him and Christ is undeniable. They are one in all its wonderful and mysterious implications which, though we cannot understand them fully, we gladly accept, and in so doing, remain faithful to God's Word.

- John 20:28, "Thomas answered and said to him, My Lord and my God!" (KJV).

No treatment of the deity of Christ would be complete without mentioning the greatest single testimony recorded in the Scriptures. John 20:28 presents that testimony.

Beginning at verse 24, the disciple Thomas is portrayed as being a thoroughgoing skeptic, in that he refused to believe that Christ had risen and appeared physically in the *same* form which had been crucified on the cross. In verse 25, Thomas stubbornly declares, "Except I shall see in his hands the print of the nails, and put my finger into the print of the nails, and thrust my hand into his side, I will not believe" (KJV). Following through the sequence of events in verses 26 and 27, we learn that the Lord appeared to Thomas together with the other disciples and presented to Thomas His body, bearing the wounds of Calvary for his inspection. This was no spirit or phantom, no "form" assumed for the occasion, as Jehovah's Witnesses maintain. This was the very body of Christ which bore the horrible imprints of excruciating torture and the pangs of an ignominious death. Here displayed before the eyes of the unbelieving disciple was the evidence which compelled him by the sheer power of its existence to adore the one who manifested the essence of deity. "Thomas answered and said to him, My Lord and my God." This was the only answer Thomas could honestly give; Christ had proved His identity; He was truly "the Lord God." Let us substantiate this beyond doubt.

Jehovah's Witnesses have vainly striven to elude this text in the Greek (*Emphatic Diaglott* and NWT), but they have unknowingly corroborated its authority beyond refutation as a brief survey of their sources will reveal.

In the *Emphatic Diaglott* (Jn 20:28, p. 396), *O Theos mou,* literally "The God of me, or my God," signifies Jehovahistic identity, and since it is in possession of the definite article, to use Jehovah's Witnesses' own argument, it must therefore mean "the only true God" (Jehovah), not "a god." On page 776 of the New World Translation (Appendix), the author of the note states, "So too John 1:1, uses O THEOS to distinguish Jehovah God from the Word (Logos) as 'a god,' 'the only begotten God' as John 1:18 calls him.' Now let us reflect on this. If Thomas called the risen Christ Jehovah (definite article), *"O Kurios mou kai o Theos mou,"* and Christ did not deny it but confirmed it by saying, "Because thou hast seen me, thou hast believed; Blessed are they not having seen yet have believed" (v. 29), then no juggling of the text in context can offset the basic thought, namely, Jesus Christ is Jehovah God!

The NWT carefully evades any explanation of the Greek text on the aforementioned point, but just as carefully inserts in the margin (p. 350) under the symbol (*) some five or six references to Christ as "a god." These references, as usual, are used abstractly, and four of them (Is 9:6; Jn 1:1; 1:18; and 10:35) have been mentioned already in previous points. The question then is, is there any other god beside Jehovah which Jehovah's Witnesses affirm to be true by their reference to Christ as "a god" (Jn 1:1; Is 9:6)? The Scriptures give but one answer. Emphatically *no!* There is no god but Jehovah. (See Is 37:16, 20; 44:68; 45:21-23.)

To be sure, there are many so-called gods in the Scriptures, but they are not gods by identity and self-existence, but by human acclamation and adoration. Satan also falls into this category, since he is the "god of this world" who holds that position only because angels and unregenerate men have accorded to him service and worship rightfully belonging to God.

The apostle Paul seals this truth with his clear-cut analysis of idolatry and false gods in 1 Corinthians 8:4-6, where he declares that an idol is nothing in itself and there is no god but Jehovah in heaven or earth, regardless of the inventions of man.

The picture then is clear: Thomas adored Christ as the risen incarnation of the Deity (Jehovah); John declared that Deity from all eternity (Jn 1:1), and Christ affirmed it irrefutably: "If ye believe not that I am [Jehovah], ye shall die in your sins" (Jn 8:24, KJV). (Cf. Ex 3:14.) Nothing can change the plain declarations of God's Word. Jesus Christ is Lord of all, and, like it or not, Jehovah's Witnesses will never destroy or remove that truth. Regardless of what is done to God's Word on earth, it remains eternal in the glory as it is written, "For ever, O LORD, thy word is settled in heaven" (Ps 119:89, KJV).

- John 5:18, "He . . . said . . . that God was his Father, making himself equal with God" (KJV).

Concluding our chapter on this vital topic is this verse that is self-explanatory. The Greek term *equal* (*ison*) cannot be debated, nor is it contextually allowable that John is here recording what the Jews said about Jesus, as Jehovah's Witnesses lamely argue. The sentence structure clearly shows that John said it under the inspiration of the Holy Spirit, and *not* the Jews! Anyone so inclined can diagram the sentence and see this for himself. No serious scholar or commentator has ever questioned it.

Jehovah's Witnesses sometimes like to claim in this passage that it states that Jesus broke the Sabbath, and they point to this as proof that it was the Jews accusing Him of breaking the Sabbath and also accusing Him of claiming equality with God. A rudimentary knowledge of New Testament Greek in the passage quickly reveals that the King James Version's translation of the word *broken* is incorrect at this point. The word quite literally means "loosed," so what really happened is that Jesus loosed the paralytic from the requirements of the Sabbath so he could carry his bed home, and this He could do because "The Son of man is Lord also of the Sabbath" (Mk 2:28). It is worth noting that the Jehovah's Witnesses *Kingdom Interlinear Translation* correctly translates the Greek word *elue* as "loosing," not breaking the Sabbath. A direct contradiction to the *New World Translation*—right across the page!

We see, then, that our Lord was equal with God the Father and the Holy Spirit in His divine nature, though inferior (as a man) by choice in His human nature as the last Adam (Jn 14:28; 1 Co 15:45-47). This text alone is of enormous value and argues powerfully for our Lord's deity.

- Hebrews 1:6, "And again, when he bringeth in the firstbegotten into the world, he saith, And let all the angels of God worship him."

This passage of Scripture is perhaps the hardest single text in all the epistles that Jehovah's Witnesses must face, especially when coupled with Luke 4:8.

When the Father brought the eternal Word into the created cosmos to become flesh (Jn 1:1, 14), He commanded all the angels of God to worship Him. The Greek word for worship (*latreuw*) leaves no room for doubt in this context; it is the same word by our Lord when refusing Satan. "Thou shalt worship the Lord [Jehovah] thy God, and him only shalt thou serve. (Lk 4:8, KJV) Exodus, chapter 20, reinforces this consistent biblical concept when God said, "Thou shalt have [or worship] no other gods before [but] me" (Ex 20:3, KJV).

Jehovah's Witnesses have no valid answer to this stunning fact. The Father commands worship of the Son, something that He expressly forbids elsewhere in Scripture, something He could only do if the Son too shares the nature of deity or the state of being God (Phil 2:5-11). If we are to believe Christ, only Jehovah can be worshiped; therefore, since He accepted worship and did not rebuke those who did so during His life on earth (see Jn 9:35-38; 20:24-29), the Son too is Jehovah God. The Bible teaches us that God cannot lie (Titus 1:2).

Jehovah's Witnesses should consider this truth, and then, with the angels, worship Him whom the Father sanctified and sent into the world, Jesus Christ the Lord of glory.

The Watchtower would have us believe that Christ was only a perfect man while on earth, but men cannot accept worship as God; and a rabbi, an office Christ held, would have rejected it instantly as blasphemy *unless* He were worthy of it; and as we have seen, only Deity was worthy. The angel whom John attempted to worship (Rev 22:8-9) forbade him to do so on the grounds that he too was a servant; "Worship Jehovah," he commanded. As a man, albeit a perfect one, Christ was made lower than the angels (Heb 2:9), and if an angel refused worship and Christ accepted it, the obvious conclusion is that our Lord was indeed Jehovah the Son, worthy of worship and honor because He was and is true Deity.

4

Refutation of Other Watchtower Dogmas

THE RESURRECTION OF CHRIST

JEHOVAH'S WITNESSES, as has been observed, deny the bodily resurrection of the Lord Jesus Christ and claim instead that He was raised a "divine spirit being," or as an "invisible spirit creature." They answer the objection that He appeared in human form by asserting that He simply took human forms as He needed them which enabled Him to be seen, for as the Logos, He would have been invisible to the human eye. In short, Jesus did not appear in the *same* form which hung upon the cross, since that body either "dissolved in gases or is preserved somewhere as a memorial to God's love."[1]

The Scriptures, however, tell a completely different story, as will be evident when their testimony is considered. Christ Himself prophesied His own bodily resurrection, and John tells us "he spake of the temple of his body" (Jn 2:21, KJV).

In John 20:25-26 the disciple Thomas doubted the literal physical resurrection of Christ only to positively declare his belief in verse 28, after Jesus (v. 27) offered His body, the same one that was crucified and still bearing the prints and spear wound, to Thomas for his examination. No one would say that the body the Lord Jesus displayed was not His crucifixion body, unless he either ignorantly or willfully denies the Word of God. It was not a body "assumed" for the time by a spiritual Christ; it was the identical form that hung on the tree—the Lord Himself; He was alive and undeniably tangible, not a "divine spirit creature." The Lord foresaw the unbelief of men in His bodily resurrection and made an explicit point of saying that He was not a spirit but

69

flesh and bones (Lk 24:39-44), and He even went so far as to
eat food to prove that He identified with humanity as well as
Deity. Christ rebuked the disciples for their unbelief in His
physical resurrection (Lk 24:25), and it was the physical resurrection that confirmed His deity, since only God could voluntarily lay down and take up life at will (Jn 10:18).*

Jehovah's Witnesses utilize, among other unconnected verses,
1 Peter 3:18 as a defense for their spiritual resurrection doctrine.
Peter declares that Christ was "put to death in the flesh, but
[made alive] by the Spirit." Obviously, He was made alive†
in the Spirit and by the Spirit of God, for the Spirit of God, the
substance of God Himself, raised up Jesus from the dead as it is
written, "But if the Spirit of him that raised up Jesus from among
the dead dwell in you, He will in like manner cause your mortal
bodies to come to life" (Ro 8:11). The meaning of the verse
then is quite clear. God did not raise Jesus a spirit but raised
Him by His Spirit, which follows perfectly John 20:27 and
Luke 24:39-44, in establishing the physical resurrection of the
Lord. Paul also states in Romans 4:24; 6:4; and 1 Corinthians
15:15, that Christ is raised from the dead, and Paul preached the
physical resurrection and return of the God-man, not a "divine
spirit being" without a tangible form. Paul also warned that if
Christ is not risen, then our faith is vain; to us who believe God's
Word, there is a man in the glory who showed His wounds as a
token of His reality and whose question we ask Jehovah's Witnesses: Has a spirit flesh and bones as well as the marks of the
cross?

THE ATONEMENT OF CHRIST

The infinite atonement of the Lord Jesus Christ is one of the
most important doctrines of the Bible, since it is the guarantee of

---

*We must never let it be forgotten that Christ prophesied not only His
resurrection but the nature of that resurrection which He said would be
bodily (Jn 2:19-21). He said He would raise up "the temple" in three
days (v. 19), and John tells us, "He spoke of the temple of His *body*"
(v. 21). The Greek word *soma* always means body, never soul(*psuche*) or
spirit (*pneuma*), and Jehovah's Witnesses are hard put to answer this; in
fact they never have.

†*The Emphatic Diaglott* renders the Greek *pneumati* as "in spirit," but
neglects to mention that it is the *agency* of the Holy Spirit being spoken of,
for it was through the operation of His power that Jesus rose again (Ro
8:11).

eternal life through the complete forgiveness of sins to whomever appropriates its cleansing power. The Old Testament clearly teaches that, "It is the *blood* that maketh an atonement for the soul." Leviticus 17:11 and Hebrews 9:22 corroborate this beyond doubt, for in truth, "Without shedding of blood is no remission." The Lord Jesus Christ became the one blood sacrifice for sin that insures everlasting life, as John said upon seeing Jesus—"Behold the Lamb of God which taketh away the sin of the world" (Jn 1:29, KJV). The apostle John, writing in Revelation 13:8, declares that the Lamb (Christ), slain from the foundation of the world, is God's own eternal sacrifice that cleanses from all sin and provides redemption for lost souls who trust in its efficacy. The writer of the epistle to the Hebrews goes to great length to show that the sacrifices of the Old Testament were types designed to show forth the coming sacrifice of Christ on Calvary (Heb 9 and 10). The Hebrew term *kaphar* (covering) and the Greek term *katallage*, which literally means "reconciliation," are used in reference to payment of an obligation or exchange. The picture then portrays Christ as bearing our sins in His own body on the tree (1 Pe 2:24) and giving us peace with God through the *blood* of His cross (Col 1:20), which blood is the everlasting covenant that is able to make us perfect, in that God through it empowers us to do His will (Heb 13:20-21). The Scriptures give vast testimony to the redeeming power of the Lamb's blood (Ro 3:25; 5:9; Col 1:14; Heb 9:22; 1 Pe 1:19; 1 Jn 1:7; Rev 5:9; 12:11) which *alone* can save and cleanse (Heb 9:22).

Charles Taze Russell resigned from a position he once held as assistant editor of a Rochester, New York, newspaper because he disagreed with the editor's view of the atonement. Whether Russell was right in that disputation, or wrong, we do not know, but his doctrine of the atonement and Jehovah's Witnesses' doctrine we do have knowledge of and know it to be completely unscriptural. Jehovah's Witnesses argue that the atonement is not wholly of God, despite 2 Corinthians 5:21, but rather half of God and half of man. Jesus, according to their argument, removed the effects of Adam's sin by His sacrifice on Calvary, but the work will not be fully completed until the survivors of Armageddon return to God through free will and become subject to the theocratic rule of Jehovah. For Jehovah's Witnesses, the full realization of the matter is reconciliation with God, which will be completed in relation to the millennial kingdom. This utterly unreasonable and illogical interpretation of Scripture does away with the validity of the "infinite atonement" unconditionally administered by God and through God for man. Russell and Jehovah's Witnesses have detracted from the blood of Christ by allowing it only partial cleansing power, but the truth still stands; it is either all-sufficient or insufficient, and if the latter be the case, man is hopelessly lost in an unconnected maze of irrelevant doctrines which postulate a finite sacrifice and by necessity, a finite god.

THE PHYSICAL RETURN OF CHRIST

Jehovah's Witnesses declare that Christ returned to the temple in 1914 and cleansed it by 1918 for judgment upon sinful men and Satan's organizations. They affirm that since He did not rise physically, neither did He return physically, nor will He.[2]

The first claim is that Jesus said "The world seeth me no more" (Jn 14:19); therefore, no mortal eye shall see Him. The second claim is the intimation that *parousia* in Matthew 24:26-28, can *only* be rendered as "presence;" therefore, Christ is now present, not coming.

These arguments are half-truths. To begin with, Thayer, who is esteemed reliable in the field of scholarship, clearly states that *parousia*, especially in the New Testament, refers to the second coming of Christ in *visible* form to raise the dead, hold the last judgment, and set up the kingdom of God.[3] Christ is present; His "presence" is always near ("I will never leave thee" Heb 13:5, KJV. "I am with you alway . . . to the consummation of the age," Mt 28:20, Scofield marg.), for as God, He is omnipresent. But that does not mean He is here physically, as the Scriptures attest He will be at the second advent. The physical return of Christ is the "blessed hope" of Christendom (Titus 2:13) and the language used to portray its visible certainty is most explicit. In Titus 2:13, the Greek word *epiphaneia* (appearing) is more correctly translated "manifestation" or "visible" from *phanero,* "to make manifest, or visible, or known."[4] The language is self-explanatory. When the Lord returns with His saints, "Every eye shall see him" (Rev 1:7). How then can Jehovah's Witnesses claim that He has already returned but is invisible? The answer is they cannot and still remain scripturally honest. To further establish these great truths, the apostle Paul, writing to Timothy in 1 Timothy 6:14, clearly states that the Lord Jesus will appear physically, by using *epiphaneia,* another form of *phanero,* which also denotes visibility or manifestation. In 1 Thessalonians 4:16-17, the Lord's return is revealed as being visible and audible, not invisible as Jehovah's Witnesses affirm contrary to Scripture.

The Old Testament bears out the physical return of Messiah, also a wonderful testimony to the consistency of God's Word. Comparing Zechariah 12:10 and 14:4 with Matthew 24:30; Acts 1:9-12; and Revelation 1:7, it is obvious that the Lord's ascension was visible for the disciples *saw* Him rise, and in like fashion (*tropos,* Greek) the angels declared He would return. Zechariah 12:10 quotes Jehovah (further proof of Christ's deity), "And they shall look upon *me* whom they have pierced" and Revelation 1:7 states that Christ is the one pierced, and *visible* to human eyes. Zechariah 14:4 reveals Christ as touching the Mount of Olives at His visible return, and the Scriptures teach that this literally corroborates the angelic proclamation of Acts 1:9-12, even to the Lord's return to the exact location of His ascension, the Mount of Olives (v. 12). The doctrine of the physical return of Christ cannot be denied in the Scriptures, unless a denial of God's Word also be entered, which would exhibit great ignorance. (See also Mt 24:23-24, 30; Lk 21:27; 2 Th 1:7-10; 2:1-2, 8.)

JEHOVAH'S WITNESSES AND HUMAN GOVERNMENT

Jehovah's Witnesses refuse to pay homage in any way to the flag of any nation or even to defend their own individual nations from assault by an enemy. Patriotism, as displayed in bearing arms, is not one of their beliefs, since they claim to be ambassadors of Jehovah, and, as such, deem themselves independent of allegiance to any government other than His. In this age of uncertainty, sincerity is a priceless gem, and no doubt Jehovah's Witnesses believe themselves sincere, but all their arguments avail nothing when in Romans 13:1-7, Paul clearly outlines the case for

human government as instituted by God. Paul goes to great
length to stress that the "higher powers" (human governmental
rulers) are allowed and sanctioned by God. As supposed followers of His Word, the Witnesses ought to heed both Christ
and Paul and "render unto Caesar what is Caesar's," which in
the context of Romans 13:1-7, clearly means subjugation to governmental rule. Paul settles the question decisively, and in conclusion, we quote his teaching:

> Let every soul be subject unto the higher powers. For there
> is no power but of God: the powers that be are ordained of
> God. Whosoever therefore resisteth the power, resisteth the
> ordinance of God: and they that resist shall receive to themselves
> damnation. For rulers are not a terror to good works, but to the
> evil. Wilt thou then not be afraid of the power? do that which
> is good, and thou shalt have praise of the same: For he is the
> minister of God to thee for good. But if thou do that which is
> evil, be afraid; for he beareth not the sword in vain: for he is
> the minister of God, a revenger to execute wrath upon him that
> doeth evil. Wherefore ye must needs be subject, not only for
> wrath, but also for conscience sake. For for this cause pay ye
> tribute also: for they are God's ministers, attending continually
> upon this very thing. Render therefore to all their dues: tribute
> to whom tribute is due; custom to whom custom; fear to whom
> fear; honour to whom honour (Ro 13:1-7, KJV).

The Existence of Hell and Eternal Punishment

The question of the existence of hell and eternal punishment
presents no problem to any biblical student who is willing to
practice honest exegesis. Jehovah's Witnesses use emotionally
loaded words such as *hell fire screechers* and *religionists* to describe the theological views of anyone who disagrees with their
philosophy. In order to understand their views, it must first be
established that their beliefs are based upon no sound or valid
knowledge of the original languages, and it should be remembered that this one factor influences practically every major
phase of semantic study. However, we will now consider this
problem in its context, and contrast it with Jehovah's Witnesses'
interpretation, which professes to have solved the problem, though
on what grounds, it is difficult to ascertain.

To begin with, grammatically, Jehovah's Witnesses use poor reasoning in their construction, and, from the evidence, seldom check the original scripts beyond the dictionary and lexicon stage. We document to prove the point and reveal this shortcoming. On pages 69 and 70 of *"Let God Be True"* (1946 edition), the following statement appears:

> If you were to translate a book from a foreign language into English and there you found the foreign word for bread 65 times, would you translate it 31 times bread, 31 times fish, and 3 times meat? Of course not. Why? Because if you did your translation would not be correct. For what is bread cannot at the same time be fish or meat and vice versa. The same holds true with the word Sheol. If Sheol is the grave, it is impossible at the same time to be a place of fiery torture and at the same time a pit.‡

To the average Jehovah's Witness, hell is Sheol, literally, "the grave," the place where mortals wait the resurrection. Their chief argument is that in translation, one word means one thing and has no area of meaning. This is a typical Jehovah's Witness approach and again reveals the linguistic failings of the organization. First of all, the very example the author of the chapter uses concerning bread, fish, and meat, is a reality in the text of the Bible, and if words do not have areas of meaning in different context, he stands accused of defaming God's Word. A little research would have revealed this truth to him, but it remains for us to clarify. In the Hebrew text, the word *lechem* is translated bread 238 times, 1 time as "feast," 21 times as "food," 1 time as "fruit," 5 times as "loaf," 18 times as "meat," 1 time as "provision," 2 times as "victuals," and 1 time as "eat." This puts to silence the argument that Sheol *always* means the grave. It is clear that it has an area of meaning which must be decided from the context, not the conjectures of misinformed authors.

In the second place, Jehovah's Witnesses have conceived of death as being unconsciousness or extinction, a definition which cannot be found in the Bible. Death, in the biblical sense, never

‡Note that this quote was from the 1946 edition of *"Let God Be True"* by J. F. Rutherford. In the revised edition of 1952, they omitted this paragraph. Was it because they realized that no Greek scholar would ever back them up?

means extinction or annihilation, and not one word, Greek or
Hebrew, in either Testament, will be found to say that it does.
Death is portrayed in the Bible as separation. "The soul that
sinneth . . . it shall be separated" (Eze 18:4) is a better rendition,
in the sense that the word conveys in consistent Old Testament
usage. (See Ec 12:7.) When Adam sinned, his soul became separated from God in the sense of fellowship; and consequently,
as a result of sin, all men die or are separated from God by
Adam's as well as their own sins (Eph 2:1; 4:18; Ro 5:15; Mt 8:22;
Col 2:13). But God has provided a reconciliation for us in the
person of His Son, and we are "born again," regenerated and rec-
onciled to God, by the sacrifice of His Son, "In whom we have
redemption through his blood, even the forgiveness of sins" (Col
1:14; cf. Jn 3:3-7, 15, 16; 2 Co 5:17-21). So then we see that death
is not extinction but conscious existence as we demonstrated in
Matthew 17:1-3, when Moses and Elijah talked with Christ.
Moses' body was dead—no one will deny; his soul was also dead,
according to Jehovah's Witnesses. Then what or who was it talking to Christ? The answer is simple. Moses, as a living soul, spoke
to Christ, and he was alive and conscious! Substantiating all this
is Christ's own declaration, "I am the resurrection, and the life;
he that believeth in me, though he were dead, yet shall he live:
and whosoever liveth and believeth on me shall never die" (Jn
11:25); therefore, death is only the separation between, not the
extinction of personalities (Is 59:1-2; see also 2 Co 5:8 and Phil 1:
21-23).

Jehovah's Witnesses claim that, "in all places where 'hell' is
translated from the Greek word *Gehenna* it means everlasting
destruction or extinction."[5]

This is indeed a bold-faced misrepresentation of the Greek
language and certainly ranks next to the "a god" fallacy of John
1:1 as an outstanding example of complete falsehood. There is
no evidence that *Gehenna* ever means "annihilation" in the New
Testament, but rather abundant evidence to the contrary. In
Matthew 5:22, Gehenna is portrayed as literally "the hell of
fire"; in 10:28, coupled with *apolesai*, "to be delivered up to eternal misery" (see Thayer, p. 64), it indicates everlasting misery,
and in Matthew 18:9, the same words corroborate 5:22, "the

hell of fire." If we are to follow through with Jehovah's Witnesses'
argument, then Gehenna simply means the smoldering furnaces of
Hinnon. But is that fire everlasting? No! For today the valley
of Hinnon is not burning; so unless Jesus meant the example for
just those living at that time, and this not even Jehovah's Witnesses will affirm, then Gehenna must be what it is, the symbol
of eternal separation in conscious torment by a flame which is
unquenchable (Is 66:24).

It is fruitless to pursue this analysis of the Greek any further,
for it must be clear from the contexts that more than the grave
or extinction is portrayed in Sheol, Hades, and Gehenna. Without
benefit of any complicated textual exegesis, we shall let God's
Word speak its own message and commit to the reader the decision as to whether eternal punishment, rather than annihilation,
is Scriptural doctrine. The following verses collectively refer to
a place of everlasting conscious torment where Satan and his
followers must remain in future everlasting wounding or misery,
separated from God's presence and "the glory of his power"
(2 Th 1:9; cf. Thayer, p. 443*a* on *olethros* and Latin *vulnerare,*
"to wound").

> And I say unto you, That many shall come from the east and
> west, and shall sit down with Abraham, and Isaac, and Jacob,
> in the kingdom of heaven. But the children of the kingdom shall
> be cast out into outer darkness: there shall be weeping and
> gnashing of teeth (Mt 8:11-12).
> And shall cast them into the furnace of fire: there shall be
> wailing and gnashing of teeth (Mt 13:42, 50).
> Then said the king to the servants, Bind him hand and foot,
> and take him away, and cast him into outer darkness; there shall
> be weeping and gnashing of teeth (Mt 22:13).
> Strive to enter in at the strait gate: for many, I say unto you,
> will seek to enter in, and shall not be able. When once the
> master of the house is risen up, and hath shut to the door, and
> ye begin to stand without, and to knock at the door, saying,
> Lord, Lord, open unto us; and he shall answer and say unto you,
> I know you not whence ye are: Then shall ye begin to say, We
> have eaten and drunk in thy presence, and thou hast taught in
> our streets. But he shall say, I tell you, I know you not whence
> ye are; depart from me, all ye workers of iniquity. There shall

be weeping and gnashing of teeth, when ye shall see Abraham,
and Isaac, and Jacob, and all the prophets, in the kingdom of
God, and you yourselves thrust out (Lk 13:24-28).

These are wells without water, clouds that are carried with a
tempest; to whom the mist of darkness is reserved for ever (2 Pe
2:17).

Raging waves of the sea, foaming out their own shame; wan-
dering stars, to whom is reserved the blackness of darkness for
ever (Jude 13).

And the third angel followed them, saying with a loud voice,
If any man worship the beast and his image, and receive his mark
in his forehead, or in his hand, The same shall drink of the wine
of the wrath of God, which is poured out without mixture into
the cup of his indignation; and he shall be tormented with fire
and brimstone . . . in the presence of the Lamb: And the smoke
of their torment ascendeth up for ever and ever: and they have
no rest day nor night, who worship the beast and his image,
and whosoever receiveth the mark of his name (Rev 14:9-11).

And the beast was taken, and with him the false prophet that
wrought miracles before him, with which he deceived them
that had received the mark of the beast, and them that wor-
shipped his image. These both were cast alive into a lake of
fire burning with brimstone (Rev 19:20).

These verses are conclusive proof that everlasting conscious
separation from God and real torment exist, and no possible confusion of terminology can change their meaning in context. Revelation 20:10 is perhaps the most descriptive of all the verses in
the Greek. John positively states that "the devil who deceived
them was cast into the lake of fire and brimstone, where the beast
and the false prophet are, and they will be tormented (*basanis-
thesontai*) day and night into the everlasting (*aionas*) of the
everlasting." The Greek word *basanizo* literally means "to torment," "to be harassed," "to torture," or "to vex with grievous
pains,"[6] and is used throughout the New Testament to denote
great pain and conscious misery, not annihilation, cessation of
consciousness, or extinction. Further proof of the reality of conscious torment, *not annihilation*, is found in the following verses
where *basanizo* is utilized to exhibit the truth of God's eternal
justice.

My servant lieth at home sick of the palsy, grievously tormented *[basanizomenos]* (Mt 8:6, KJV).

Art thou come hither to torment *[basanisai]* us before the time? (Mt 8:29, KJV).

Torment *[basanisas]* me not (Mk 5:7, KJV).

He [the believer in the beast] shall be tormented *[Basanistheaseta]* with fire and brimstone in the presence of the holy angels, and in the presence of the Lamb: And the smoke of their torment rises up into the everlasting of the everlasting; and they have no intermission, cessation, or relief, day and night who worship the Beast and his image and if any one receive the mark of his name (Rev 14:10-11, KJV). (See Thayer, p. 40*b*, on *anapausis*.)

The Scriptures clearly teach eternal conscious punishment and torment for those who reject Christ as Lord, and the language of the texts leaves no room for doubt that the apostles intended that confirmation. Jehovah's Witnesses think God a "fiend" because He executes eternal righteous judgment. They make much to-do about God being love but forget that because He is love, He is also justice and must require infinite vengeance from anyone who treads underfoot the precious blood of Christ who is the Lamb slain for lost sinners from the foundation of the world. Death is not extinction, hell is not an illusion, and everlasting conscious punishment is a terrifying reality of God's infinite justice upon the souls of unbelieving men. The apostle Paul summed up this certainty in Romans 2:5-9, when he declared that God's indignation (*thumos*) and wrath (*orges*) are upon all who work unrighteousness. These two words have identical usage in Revelation 14:10, where John speaks of the eternal torment of those who serve the beast, "That wine of the wrath (*orges*) of God, which is mingled undiluted in the cup of His indignation (*thumou*)." So then the picture is clear. God is both love and justice, and it is not He who condemns man, but man who condemns himself as it is written—"For by thy words thou shalt be justified, and by thy words thou shalt be condemned" (Mt 12:37).

Jehovah's Witnesses exhibit their lack of knowledge as to what fundamental Christians believe when speaking of the "religious theologians," they declare, "But do they not say that Satan the Devil with his demons are in hell keeping up the fires and making it hard for those who are therein? Yes, that is what is taught by

the religious leaders."[7] It is nonsense to suppose that the devil
and his demons "are in hell keeping up the fires," and no responsible clergyman or Christian would make so childish a statement.
To claim that "religionists" teach such doctrines is to reveal ignorance of the facts. Further comment is not justified. Further
examination is superfluous.

Luke 16:19-31 is claimed to be a parable in the text by Jehovah's Witnesses, but nowhere is this substantiated in Luke's account. It is pure conjecture. Jehovah's Witnesses claim that the
"parable" portrays a coming event which was fulfilled in 1918.
The rich man represents the clergy and Lazarus the "faithful
body of Christ." The clergy is constantly tormented by the truth
proclaimed through the faithful remnant.[8] Comment on this
eisegetical travesty is senseless, since Jehovah's Witnesses twist
the Scripture to suit their own ends regardless of the textual
background. The Lord Jesus in this account portrayed the condition of a lost soul (the rich man) who rejected God, and the
beggar who partook of the Lord's mercy. The rich man went
into conscious torment after physical death (*basanois*), verse 24,
and even proclaimed his spiritual conscious anguish (*odunomai*),
"I am being tormented" (see Thayer, p. 438*b*). There can be no
doubt, he was suffering and knew it. Jehovah's Witnesses believe
that in order to suffer, you must exist physically, but this is naive
to say the least, since souls suffer, as is demonstrated in this
account. It must also be remembered that Christ, in parables,
never used personal names, such as *Lazarus*.

We must conclude then that Luke's account is a record of an
actual case, an historical fact in which a soul suffered after death
and was conscious of that torment. Regardless of what conjectures are injected at this point, the conclusion is sure: there is
conscious punishment after death; and whether it is accepted by
Jehovah's Witnesses, it still remains a scriptural doctrine substantiated by God's Word.

SATAN, THE DEVIL

Jehovah's Witnesses maintain a guarded orthodoxy toward the
doctrine of Satan in the Scriptures and deviate in only one major

place where they can be called to reckoning. In "*Let God Be True*") pp. 55 and 56, they declare in essence that "the end of Satan is complete annihilation." This fallacy stems from their insistence on interpreting physical death as extinction as well as the second death of Revelation. Why they cannot do this has already been discussed, and Revelation 20:10 answers the problem of Satan's eternal destiny more than adequately. John declares that he and his (they) will be *tormented* (*basanithesontai*) day and night into the everlasting, but not annihilated. Figurative analysis is allowable where the language has broad meanings, but the area of meaning of *basanizo* (torment) is definitely limited as is *aionas* (everlasting), so any far-fetched interpretations cannot long endure under the grammar of the language. Satan will suffer eternally in real torment, not in literal fire that consumes, since he is a spirit and must suffer spiritual punishment.

In Ezekiel 28:16-19, Jehovah's Witnesses again maintain Satan's annihilation,[9] but in the light of the Scriptures before discussed, the area of meanings of the Hebrew words must be considered. The word for "destroy" ('*ABAD*) does not convey the meaning of annihilation or extinction. The term here used may be validly rendered "to reckon as lost, given up as lost, or cast away" (cf. Ec 3:6b, and also Gesenius' *Hebrew-English Lexicon*). If Ezekiel 28:19 is as translated, "never shalt thou *be* anymore," the Hebrew word '*AYIN*[10] may properly be rendered "to fail" or "to be gone," *not* to cease to exist (cf. 1 Ki 20:40; Is 44:12). The use of '*AYIN* in Hebrew sentence structure is the standard means employed when negating noun clauses. In 1 Kings 20:40, for example, where the man is spoken of as "gone," the term '*AYIN* is utilized to show the man's absence or escape, *not* his extinction. If Jehovah's Witnesses persist in their annihilation doctrine where Satan is concerned, they must also believe that the man was annihilated, and the context rules out that interpretation as absurd. The picture then is clear, in the light of language interpretation. Satan *must* and *will* endure everlasting torment with his followers, and to this truth, God's Word bears irrefutable testimony.

MAN THE SOUL, HIS NATURE AND DESTINY

In examining this problem, one cannot escape the confusion of terms utilized by Jehovah's Witnesses to substantiate their argument that the soul is not an eternal entity. To carry this argument to any great length is foolish, for the Hebrew word (*NEPHESH*) and the Greek (*psuche*) possess great areas of meaning impossible to fathom without exhaustive exegesis of the original sources. The root of the problem lies in Jehovah's Witnesses' misconception of the soul as merely a principle of life, not an entity. The Bible clearly teaches in numerous places that the soul departs at the death of the body, that it is not destroyed by physical death, and that it can be restored by God at His discretion (Gen 35:18; 1 Ki 17:21-22; Rev 6:9-11).

In an exegetical study, it is impossible to emphasize too much the importance of defining terms, and in the problem at hand, it is of the utmost importance. Therefore, before we can decide who or what has immortality, we must know what the term *immortality* itself means. Due to the evolution of any language, we must realize that the area of meanings of words changes as time goes on. The English word *immortal* has, among others, a peculiar meaning of "not mortal." However, in most circles and also in theology, the word generally carries the meaning of "exemption from death." The question that will arise then is, When the Scriptures use the term *immortal*, is this definition all that is meant? Contrary to the belief of some, there is *no reference* in Scripture that can be given to show that man or his soul is immortal.

To go even one step farther, there is nothing in Scripture that states anything or anyone is now immortal, but God Himself. Let us analyze this problem. There are two words in the Greek text that are translated "immortality." The first is *athanasia*, and it appears three times and is translated "immortality" each time. The other term is *aphthartos*, and is translated "immortality" twice and "incorruption" four times. Now let us examine the use of these words. The word *athanasian* is used in 1 Timothy 6:16 and is speaking of God, "Who *alone* has immortality (*athanasian*) dwelling in the light which *no man* can approach unto." In 1 Corinthians 15:53-54, we again have *athanasia* used twice, but in the same verse we have *aphthartos* used twice also. Paul here is speaking of the second coming of Christ, and declares (v. 53), "For this corruption must put on incorruption *aphtharsian,* and this mortal must put on immortality (*athanasian*)." "So when this corruption *shall have put on incorruption* (*aphtharsian*), and this mortal *have put on* immortality (*athanasian*) *then* shall be brought to pass the saying that is written, *Death* is swallowed up in victory" (v. 54). We see here that in the two places where *athanasian* is used in reference to man, it is an immortality to be given in the future, not one possessed at the present time.

Similarly, when an *aphtharsian* is used here and in Romans 2:7, something sought for, and 1 Peter 1:4, "reserved in heaven for you" (KJV), it is speaking of the incorruption of man to be given at some future date, not possessed at the present time. Only when immortality or incorruption is used with God is it in the present tense (Ro 1:23; 1 Ti 1:17; 6:16). Therefore, to say that the saints are immortal (if by immortality we mean *athanasian* or *aphtharsian*), we are not scriptural. We must say the saints *will be* immortal. Also, in 1 Corinthians 15:53-54, this immortality (*athanasian*) and this incorruption (*aphtharsian*) *will be put on* (*endusetai*) as one puts on a garment. Just as Paul exhorts us to put on (*endusasthe*) Christ (Ro 13:14; Gal 3:27), the armor of light (Ro 13:12), the new man (Eph 4:24), and the armor, or panoply, of God (Eph 6:11), we must conclude then that *athanasian* or *aphtharsian* have a larger and broader meaning than to be "everlasting." It must be seen that immortality and incorruption, *when given,* will mean a change, not simply the giving and receiving of the attribute—"exemption from death." Jehovah's Witnesses have badly misconstrued the usage of immortality; and that error, coupled with their famous practice of term-switching, has resulted in confusion and poor exegesis.

Now as to the eternity of the human soul, we must consult the existing language sources. When we use the term *eternal* in association with the soul of man, we mean that the human soul *after* its creating by God will (future) exist somewhere into the eternal, into the everlasting. Since there is only one place where one can find pure information on the eternal existence of the soul—the revelation which God, who created the soul, has given to man, namely His Word—let us turn to it and consider therein His revealed will.

Revelation does show, first, that God can be known, and, second, that man's soul is eternal. In Hebrews 1:1, we read, "God, who at sundry times and in divers manners spake in time past unto the fathers by the prophets, Hath in these last days spoken unto us by his Son, whom he hath appointed heir of all things, by whom also he made the worlds" (KJV). All through history, God has manifested Himself to man in different ways, and at no time in history has man been left without a witness of God. In the Old Testament, God manifested Himself and His will to man by the prophets, visions, and direct oral contact. However, when the fullness of time was come, God sent forth His Son in the likeness of sinful flesh and completed His progressive revelation. Man, since the time of his creation upon the earth, has always been able to know God and His will, if he so desired; and consequently, since the day of Adam, men who know not God are without excuse.

God's revelation is not only a manifestation of God to man, but it also is the answer to the questions, Where did man come from? Is he a spiritual as well as natural being? What is his worth? and Where is he going?

God's revelation shows that man is a creation of God, created in God's spiritual image (Gen 1:26; 5:1; 1 Co 11:7). He was created to have preeminence over other creatures (Gen 1:28; Ps 8:6; 82:6; Mt 6:26; 12:12). He is definitely a spiritual being (Job 32:8; Ec 12:7; Ac 7:59). He is an object of God's love (Jn 3:16; Rev 1:5). He sinned and lost God's favor (Gen 3:1-19). Adam's sin passed upon all mankind (Ro 5:12). God sent His Son to redeem man (Jn 3:16). This redemption is by the vicarious death of Christ (Mt 26:28; Ac 20:28; Ro 5:9; Col 1:20; Heb 9:14; 1 Pe 1:18-19; 1 Jn 1:7; Rev 1:5; 7:14). This salvation is obtained by a new birth through faith in Jesus Christ (Jn 3:3-16).

We must then conclude that since "God is a Spirit" (Jn 4:24, KJV) and as such is incorporeal, He must have imparted to man a spiritual nature created in His own image, or else Genesis 1:26 is not meaningful.

Now the question arises, If Jesus redeems those who accept

His salvation, what is the difference between those who are redeemed and those who are not? It is clear that redemption is not simply favor with God here upon earth. This brings us to the scriptural teaching of the eternal existence of the soul. First, there is much evidence that the soul does exist as a conscious entity after it departs from the body, and there is no scriptural evidence to the contrary. The apostle Paul longed to die (depart) "and be with Christ which is far better" (Phil 1:21-23) and taught that the absence of a Christian's spirit from his body placed him "at home with the Lord" (2 Co 5:8). See also 1 Samuel 28: 15-20 where the spirit of Samuel appears to Saul to announce Jehovah's judgment.

In Matthew 17, we see Moses and Elijah on the mount of transfiguration with Christ, and communing with Him, yet we know that Moses had been physically dead for centuries, and no record of his resurrection exists in Scripture.§

In Luke 16:19-31 (and this is not a parable), Jesus shows the difference between the state of the soul of the redeemed and the state of the soul of the wicked after death. In Revelation 6:9-10, the souls of those who had been martyred for Christ cry out for vengeance. In 2 Corinthians 5:1-9, Paul makes it clear that to be absent from the body is to be consciously "present" or "at home" with the Lord. But the Scriptures go even further, for they speak of a resurrection of the body (Job 19:25; 1 Co 15:35-57; 1 Th 4:16-17). In 1 Corinthians 15:35-49, is found the answer to this question which the Jehovah Witnesses are laboring under, that is (v. 35), "How are the dead raised up? and with what body do they come?" Notice that in verse 36 Paul addresses those who labor under this question as "Thou fool."

Now that we have considered the problem of the soul's existence after death, and the resurrection of the body, we find that Scripture is clear in its teaching that those who reject God's salvation will suffer throughout eternity in outer darkness (Mt 8:11-12;

§Jehovah's Witnesses claim that this was a vision, not a "real" evidence of the soul's existence beyond the grave, and they point to Mt 17:9, where the English rendition of the Greek (*orama*) is "vision." However, this Greek term literally reads, "that which is seen—a spectacle" (see Thayer, p. 451), not merely "vision"; hence the occurrence was real and therefore sufficient evidence to indicate the conscious survival of the soul or spirit after physical death.

13:42-50; 22:13; Lk 13:24-28; 2 Pe 2:17; Jude 13; Rev 14:9-11; 19:20), and those who accept God's salvation will dwell with Christ throughout eternity in joy and peace (Lk 20:36; Jn 14:1-3; 17:24; 1 Th 4:17; Rev 22:5). Here is revealed what we believe is the true meaning of the scriptural terms *immortality* and *incorruption* (*athanasian, aphtharsian*). We must also realize that these words do not apply to God the Father in the same sense that they apply to God the Son. When we come "with" Him from heaven (1 Th 4:14), we shall be made like Him in the sense that we shall have a soul and body *incapable* of sin, not earthly but heavenly. We shall put on *aphtharsian* and *athanasian* and abide with Christ into the eternal.

We have now presented what we feel is sufficient evidence to refute some of the major conflicts between Christian theology and that of the Jehovah's Witnesses; we have shown that man has an eternal soul and shall abide somewhere either in conscious joy or sorrow eternally, and that those who believe and trust in Christ as their personal Saviour will "put on" that immortality when Jesus returns.

Regarding the Jehovah's Witnesses, we can only say as Paul said to the Corinthians in 2 Corinthians 4:3-4 (KJV), "But if our gospel be hid, it is hid to them that are lost: In whom the God of this world hath blinded the minds of them which believe not, lest the light of the glorious gospel of Christ, who is the image of God, should shine unto them"; and as he again states in 2 Thessalonians 2:10b-11, "Because they received not the love of the truth, that they might be saved. And for this cause God shall send them strong delusion, that they should believe a lie" (KJV).

A study of this problem will reveal that man does possess an eternal, immaterial nature which was fashioned to occupy an everlasting habitation whether in conscious bliss or torment. This then is the nature and certain destiny of man.

In conclusion, we offer the following partial list of references to the soul and spirit of man as drawn from the Old and New Testaments which will, we believe, furnish the reader with ample evidence that man is not just a combination of body and breath, forming a living soul, as the Jehovah's Witnesses teach, but rather a soul, or spirit, possessing a corporeal form.

The Hebrew equivalent for soul as used in the Old Testament is *nephesh*, and for spirit *ruach*. The Greek equivalent for soul is *psuche* and for spirit *pneuma*.

1. The spirit is separate from the body (Mt 10:28; Lk 8:55; 1 Th 5:23; Heb 4:12; Rev 16:3), that is, it exists independent of material form (Zec 12:1).
2. A soul or spirit departs at the death of the form (Gen 35:18; Ec 3:21; 21:7).
3. The soul is conscious after death (1 Sa 28:18-19; Mt 17:3; Gal 6:8; Rev 6:9-11).
4. Stephen had a spirit which he committed to Christ at his death (Ac 7:59).
5. There is definitely a spirit and soul of man (Is 57:16).
6. The spirit, the soul of man, does that which only a personality can do; it "wills" [*prothumon*] (Mt 26:41); it also has the faculty of knowing (1 Co 2:11).
7. We are instructed to worship in the spirit (Jn 4:23) since God is a Spirit.
8. The spirit belongs to God, and we are instructed to glorify Him in it (1 Co 6:20).
9. Christ is with our spirit (2 Ti 4:22), for the spirit is the life of the body (Ja 2:26).
10. We are born of God's Spirit, and as such are spirit ourselves (Jn 3:5-6).

These references will suffice to show that the immaterial nature of man is far from such a combination as the Watchtower maintains.

THE KINGDOM OF HEAVEN

The human soul, marred and stained as it is by the burden of inherent sin, seeks constant escape from the reality of that sin and the sure penalty due because of it. Once the reality of eternal punishment is clouded by idealistic concepts of everlasting bliss without the fear of personal reckoning, the soul can relax, so to speak, and the sinner, unconscious of the impending doom, God's justice, rests secure in the persuasion that "God is love." Laboring under this delusion, it is no wonder that Jehovah's Witnesses can so calmly construct the kingdom of heaven, for to them, biblical judgment or God's infinite justice does not exist and eternal retribution is only an invention of "hell fire screechers."

The biblical kingdom of heaven has many aspects, none of which includes the invented hierarchal construction so vividly outlined in Watchtower books. In Luke 17:20-21, the Lord reveals the kingdom of heaven as within the believer in one aspect but clearly states that the heavenly aspect will be visible and observable at His return (vv. 23-26). In Matthew 13, the Lord Jesus portrays the kingdom of heaven symbolically in parables; yet always it is pictured as reality, not invisible phantom government. Jehovah's Witnesses arrive at the year 1914 as the end of the Gentile times and the beginning of the reign of the invisible heavenly King, Christ Jesus. How they arrived at this arbitrary date, is in itself worthy of another chapter, but valuable evidence to the effect that Pastor Russell formulated the whole hoax is obtainable from the July 15, 1950, copy of *The Watchtower*, where on pages 216-17, the following statements are found.

Away back in 1880 the columns of "The Watch Tower" had called notice to Bible Chronology marking A.D. 1914 as the year for the 2,520 year period to end referred to by Jesus as "the times of the Gentiles" in his prophecy on the world's end (Luke 21:24). In harmony with this it was expected that in 1914 the kingdom of God by Christ Jesus in the heavens would be fully established, while the world would be involved in an unprecedented time of trouble. The religious leaders and the systems of Christendom were all set to laugh at Brother Russell and his fellow witnesses of Jehovah over failure of his announced predictions concerning A.D. 1914. But it was no laughing matter when, at the end of July, World War I broke out and by October it had become global in its scope. Christendom's religious mouths were silenced at this frightening turn of events, but not Brother Russell's. October 1, 1914, on taking his place at the breakfast table in the Brooklyn Bethel dining-room, he in a strong voice denoting conviction announced:

"The Gentile Times have ended."

Knowing that the world had now reached the time for its dissolution he refused to heed the plea of U. S. President Wilson for all clergymen and preachers to join in nation wide prayer for peace.

To follow through Jehovah's Witnesses interpretation of the kingdom, it is necessary to understand that only 144,000 faithful servants will rule with King Jesus in the heavenly sphere. They quote Revelation 7:4 and 14:1, 3 but neglect to notice that the 144,000 are of the tribes of Israel (Jews), 12,000 of each tribe, and are in no sense to be construed as anything else. This is not figurative; this is actual, since the tribes are listed by name. To follow out their own argument, Jehovah's Witnesses must believe that only 144,000 Jewish members of their organization will be privileged to reign with Christ Jesus. But by far the most telling point against their position is in verses 9, 13, 14, and 17. The "great multitude" (v. 9) are in heaven before Jehovah's throne (vv. 10, 13, 14, 15, 17). No man can number them, so they are *not* the 144,000, but tribulation saints (v. 14). They are resurrected beings in white robes (v. 13) serving Jehovah before His throne forever (v. 15), and Christ too is with them. This demolishes the myth that only 144,000 will make up the "heavenly class," or "bride of Christ." The Watchtower evades this point constantly. The texts are then clear that Israel after the flesh is mentioned and not spiritual symbolism; therefore, the 144,000 conjecture pertaining to kingdom rule, as advanced by Jehovah's Witnesses, is exposed by the light of scriptural truth.

In concluding this point, it is imperative to remember that there can be no kingdom without the King, and the Scripture is clear when it states that the true kingdom will be instituted at Christ's visible return.

The Old and New Testaments corroborate each other in establishing the certainty of the visible return and reign of Christ. (Cf. Is 11 and 12, Eze 37:20-28; Zec 12:10; 14:4; Mt 24:26-31; and Lk 17:22-37.) Jehovah's Witnesses unknowingly fulfill the prophecy of Christ in Matthew 24:23-31, where the Lord warns of false Christs and prophets who shall say Christ is here, Christ is there (in the desert, in the secret places, etc.), and shall deceive many with their deceit. Jehovah's Witnesses say He is here now, but the Lord said that He would be visible at His return, and every eye should see Him (Rev 1:7; cf. Mt 24:27-30). How then can we doubt His testimony when He Himself has said: "And the sign of the Son of Man will then appear in Heaven and all the tribes of the earth will wail—and they will *see* [visible] the Son of Man coming on the clouds of Heaven, with great majesty and power" (Mt 24:30).

To this we can only say with John, "Even so, come, Lord Jesus" (Rev 22:20).

5

Jehovah's Witnesses' Propaganda and Blood Transfusion

No EVALUATION of the Jehovah's Witness movement would be complete without a survey of the Society's vast publishing operation, which, since its conception in 1879, has been largely responsible for the tremendous growth and development of the Russellite Watchtower. Early in his career, Pastor Russell realized the importance of advertising as a means of religious promotion, a fact testified to by the emphasis Russell placed on circulating his sermons and various writings (over 15,000,000 volumes of *Studies in the Scriptures* alone). Inability to buy Russell's writings never deterred the pastor, and he was known for constantly giving his books away at no charge. Whatever else might be said about Charles Taze Russell, let it never be said that he was not a brilliant businessman, who exploited the ancient Arian heresy*, mixed with his own paraphrased interpretations of the Bible, into a million-dollar monument to his own memory. After the demise of "the great paraphraser," Judge J. F. Rutherford, his worthy successor, took up the Pastor's flickering torch and hurled it with unyielding force and renewed energy into the ranks of those he charged with making religion "a racket." Under the Judge's leadership, there was erected in Brooklyn, New York (1929), a large well-equipped printing plant (described in the first chapter), and until its recent sale to a Christian corporation,

*A system of heretical theology originated by Arius of Alexandria in the third century A.D., which taught that Jesus Christ was not God incarnate but merely a created being, the first and greatest creation of Jehovah, the Father.

91

a well-staffed radio station, WBBR (now WPOW), which was set in operation at Staten Island. From this printing plant billions of pieces of literature have flowed to the four corners of the globe in more than 160 languages, carrying the Russellite gospel of a demigod savior, and advocating a blind acceptance of Jehovah of the Watchtower, the Russell-Rutherford myth. Prior to Judge Rutherford's death in January 1942, the Society featured regular messages from its leader, which WBBR broadcast by transcription and, on rare occasions, in person. Countless phonograph records were also distributed by the Society, thus making the Judge's "inspiring" assaults upon "organized religion" available to everybody willing (and at times even unwilling) to listen. Until 1943 and even later, loyal Witnesses could almost always be found in possession of small portable phonographs and a good supply of the Judge's recordings, which they peddled from door to door while attempting to sell for a contribution of twenty-five cents, the writings of "the theocracy's earthly leader." In 1944 the Witnesses possessed 1,000 sound trucks, which blared the theocratic message to all within hearing distance, especially at large rallies and in rural territories, where the prospective converts needed to be attracted to a central location for kingdom preaching. The Watchtower lets no grass grow under its feet, as the saying goes, and is busier than ever where general propaganda is concerned.

At the beginning of this study, the authors had the privilege of talking extensively with Dr. Herbert H. Stroup, then professor of sociology at Brooklyn College, whose superb sociological evaluations of the Jehovah's Witness movement contributed greatly to our present effort.† During our discussion, Dr. Stroup remarked constantly on the growth and scope of the cult's operations since he completed his study, and he made no secret of his opinion that sociologically, they offered even more promise of rapid multiplication in the future. Dr. Stroup also confirmed our opinion that the Jehovah's Witness movement appeals chiefly to a certain type of individual who, lacking a strong feeling of security, finds a definite psychological outlet in an organization which sets its face against *all* religions, and offers a paradise of pleasure to the

†See Herbert Hewitt Stroup, *The Jehovah's Witnesses* (New York: Columbia U., 1945).

lonely and the downtrodden of the earth. Truly, in the words of the *American* magazine, they are "peddlers of paradise." The *Reader's Digest* (February 1947) reported that less than one percent of the Witnesses had a college education, and only a comparatively few had completed high school. Further, more current, surveys indicate scant improvement. Less than five percent have completed college, and less than half have finished high school. By calling these facts to public attention, we desire to show the educational denominator to which the Watchtower appeals. Of course, there are professional men in the movement, among them mystery novelist Mickey Spillane, who once allegedly renounced his writings for the privilege of kingdom preaching. However, these conversions are rare among the Witnesses, and only serve to show that even an accomplished professional can fall prey to the theocratic "pot of gold" offered by the perpetually zealous publisher of the theocracy. At one of their many Bible studies we attended, we produced evidence that Pastor Russell authored the Watchtower's theological system. The newer members of the group knew nothing about Russell at all and were visibly shaken when we reviewed his record. However, to all appearances, our mission was not a welcome one, and we left their company later in the evening with a deep sense of our failure where reaching these victims of the Russellite gospel was concerned and an earnest desire to be better equipped in our contest for the faith.

All in the Society are tireless in their propaganda efforts; what a testimony to our lethargy in apologetics. The Witnesses are also quick to follow up a prospective convert. Some time ago, one of the authors sent for a copy of the *Emphatic Diaglott*, the Society's Greek interlinear translation of the New Testament. Shortly after we received the text, a well-dressed, polite, young man called at our home and desired to discuss our reasons for ordering the *Diaglott*. Were we interested in the Society, he asked, and could he help us to know the truth? This first meeting touched off a serious debate on such doctrines as the deity of Christ, the Trinity, and the resurrection, all of which he denied, as a good Jehovah's Witness always will. Though we presented many arguments which he was at a loss to answer, our zealous missionary beat a hasty retreat promising to come back with the answers in two weeks. When, at the end of two weeks, he failed to return, we contacted him and pressed the previously made engagement, which resulted in his return the following week. At this meeting, we introduced him to Robert Moreland, then instructor in Greek and Hebrew at Shelton College, who volunteered to aid him in his translation of John 1:1, Colossians 2:9, John 8:58, and other texts the Witnesses mistranslate in order to substantiate their unorthodox doctrines. Our Witness friend was completely floored by Professor Moreland's exegesis of the Greek and Hebrew and admitted that he could not refute it. Pressing our opportunity in a spirit of Christian love, we preached the true gospel, void of Russell's interpretations, and for the first time in our talks, saw it go unchallenged. The young Witness left our company never to return, but refused to renounce the movement, though he admitted that he could not refute the proofs of its theological shortcomings. This incident, more than any one thing, has led the authors to believe that scriptural facts, honestly presented and substantiated, can halt the flow of Russellite propaganda in its tracks and, more than this, sow the indestructible seeds of God's Word, which Isaiah the prophet declares "will never return to Him void and will prosper."

In recent years, various newspapers and periodicals have mentioned in no small proportions another of the Jehovah's Witnesses' propaganda efforts, namely, the peculiar views they hold in regard to transfusions of human blood. Since the Witnesses masquerade as "a sect of Fundamentalists" and call themselves by the name of Christian, it behooves those who do represent orthodox Christianity to set the record straight. The authors spent considerable time in research on one of the Witnesses' strangest doctrines, that of blood transfusion. We visited the Watchtower publication plant in Brooklyn, interviewed various Witnesses on their transfusion dogma, and collected all of their writings available on the subject. We, therefore, write this section fully understanding the Witnesses' views from firsthand knowledge, not hearsay.

Following the death of Judge J. F. Rutherford (prophet, priest, and official voice of the Watchtower theocratic organization), in

January 1942, a new doctrine began to develop under the suc-
ceeding administration headed by Nathan H. Knorr. The Judge,
like the pastor, gradually faded into the Russellite shadows, and
a new doctrine, foreign even to the Judge's prolific pen, crept into
the theocratic fold. By some method of reasoning not connected
with known processes of logical thought, the Watchtower sud-
denly "discovered" that blood transfusions were biblically forbidden. Unhampered by the fact that the Bible never speaks on
the subject (for it was completely unknown in that era), *The
Watchtower* announced (July 1, 1945), in an article entitled,
"Sanctity of Blood," that it was a violation of Jehovah's covenant
to transfuse human blood, even if the life of the patient was at
stake. This new "revelation" of the Russellite prophets caused
no end of protest from medical men, who knew that human life
was in jeopardy and that they were sworn to preserve it. Of
course, we would agree with Jehovah's Witnesses on the issue
involved if it were based on scriptural grounds, but in no sense
can their arguments be supported from the Bible. Russellite
thought on the subject seems to be revealed in their odd interpretation of the Levitical priesthood rulings on the office of sacrificial
blood. Let us then consider and weigh the entire teaching of the
Bible on this matter, not just isolated verses the Witnesses have
seized upon because they suit their temporary need for a new
propaganda weapon.

In *Awake* magazine (May 22, 1951, p. 3), Jehovah's Witnesses
quote Genesis 9:4, Leviticus 3:17; 7:27; and 17:10, 11, 14, and
maintain that these texts support their refusal to recognize human
blood transfusions. We shall now examine these references and
see if their contentions are textually valid.

"Flesh with the life thereof, which is the blood thereof, shall
ye not eat" (Gen 9:4, as quoted in *Awake*). This verse, as it
appears in context, has not the remotest connection with human
blood, much less transfusions. In the previous verse of the same
chapter, Jehovah clearly tells Noah that He is speaking in reference to animals and *their* flesh and that he should not eat *their*
blood. God told Noah that animal flesh was for food with but one
provision—that he *eat not of the blood*. "Every moving thing that
liveth shall be meat for you; even as the green herb have I given

you all things. But flesh with the life thereof, which is the blood thereof, *shall ye not eat*" (Gen 9:3-4, KJV).

Jehovah's Witnesses go on further in their article ("Children—Do They Belong to Parent or to the State?") to declare that Leviticus 3:17 and 7:27 forbid blood transfusions. Once again, the Russellites misinterpret the meaning of the Levitical ordinance pertaining to the sacrifices and burnt offerings. "It shall be a perpetual statute for your generations throughout all your dwellings, that ye *eat* neither fat nor blood" (Lev 3:17, KJV). "Whatsoever soul it be that *eateth* any manner of blood, even that soul shall be cut off from his people" (Lev 7:27, KJV).

Little need be said for these two verses in the way of a thorough explanation. The third chapter of Leviticus clearly speaks of sacrifices and offerings *to be eaten as food*, and speaks of animal blood being *eaten, not* human blood being transfused. Leviticus 7:27 again refers to animal blood as food eaten and digested with no possible reference to transfusion. Rounding out their expedition into the Old Testament, Jehovah's Witnesses set upon the seventeenth chapter of Leviticus as an argument against blood transfusions, but fail to mention the context of the verses they quote. *Awake* lists the references as Leviticus 17:10, 11, 14, but strangely omit verses 12 and 13 which clarify the texts. Verse 13 reads, "And whatsoever man there be of the children of Israel, or of the strangers that sojourn among you, which hunteth and catcheth any *beast or fowl* that may be *eaten;* he shall even pour out the blood thereof, and cover it with dust" (KJV).

This text clearly shows, as does the entire context of the chapter, that it refers *primarily* to animal's blood and eating, since cannibalism was expressly forbidden under the commandment, "Thou shalt not do murder," as well as in other teachings of the Scripture. As a matter of interest, it might also be noted that whenever human sacrifice is mentioned in the Bible, it is always declared abominable to the Lord. Israel was expressly forbidden to kill, much less eat one another, under penalty of immediate judgment, as it is written, "Whoso sheddeth man's blood, by man shall his blood be shed: for in the image of God made he man" (Gen 9:6, KJV).

Jehovah's Witnesses cite many more passages from the Old

Testament against the eating of blood. In the New Testament, they continue. The writer of the article in *Awake* lists Acts 15: 19, 20, 28, 29, and 21:25, to corroborate from the New Covenant the Old Testament teaching on the eating of blood. But now let us look at what the Witnesses are trying to prove and see if the point is valid.

First, orthodox Christianity recognizes and observes the rulings on the *eating* of blood as found in the Old and New Testaments. However, we cannot agree with the conclusion drawn by Jehovah's Witnesses. The Watchtower insists that the transfusion of human blood through the veins is as much feeding the body as eating through the mouth. This is indeed a clever deduction, but in view of the Scripture's teaching, it cannot stand up and medically is absurd. Eating involves digestion, and transfused blood is not digested!

In the Old Testament, Jehovah forbade as unclean, eating the blood of animals and likewise the blood of man. Blood transfusion is, in a technical sense, the "feeding" of the body when disease or anemia lower the blood count and "starves" the vital organs. It does not involve in any possible sense the sacrifice of life, the impairment of another's health, or the violation of a code of sacrificial laws as found in the Old Testament. Jehovah's Witnesses cannot produce one single verse of Scripture in reference to the blood of man, either in transfusion or ceremonial sacrifice, which in any way could be construed as an argument against saving another's life. When one gives a transfusion, it is not a sacrifice of life, and the *eating* of forbidden blood, but a transference of life from one person to another, a gift of strength offered in a spirit of mercy and charity. Anyone who has beheld another dying for lack of blood and has witnessed the disintegration of human life can appreciate the great good blood transfusions have accomplished on the whole. Of course, there are cases where infection (hepatitis particularly) or even death occur, but the percentage is so small that it does not warrant comparison. Nevertheless, Jehovah's Witnesses persist with ever heightening waves of propaganda to condemn all who sanction or participate in blood transfusions. Say the Witnesses, "So, whether one eats congealed blood in unbled meat, or drinks it at a slaughterhouse, or takes it by intravenous feeding at a hospital, it is still a violation of divine restriction that forbids taking blood into the system."[1]

This is only one of the many dogmatic assertions by the Witnesses that they are *the* authority on Jehovah's Word, the Bible. Despite the fact that they will not answer criticism on this point and many others in biblical theology, they persist in playing the fountain of truth and Jehovah's theocratic organization.

"Jesus poured His (Blood) out as a ransom price, not as a transfusion,"[2] the Watchtower declares, and shouts all others to silence with myriads of tracts, pamphlets, and books.

The confused Watchtower has fought blood transfusion even to the high courts of our land. On October 31, young Jonathan Sheton was taken from his mother, Hazel, a confirmed Jehovah's Witness, who was willing to offer up the life of her child who was suffering from a ruptured appendix, rather than submit him to blood transfusion.[3] This unfortunate woman did not take her position because the Bible taught it, but because the Watchtower Bible and Tract Society *said* the Bible taught it. This is a far different matter.

On April 17, 1951, Mrs. Rhoda Labrenz of Chicago, another ardent Jehovah's Witness, refused her needy daughter Cheryl Lynn a blood transfusion on the grounds that "We can't break Jehovah's law."[4] It is indeed a sad turn of events when a mother will abandon her child to possible death simply because the Watchtower of Jehovah's Witnesses *says this* is Jehovah's law! A case similar to this one, but one with bitter and tragic results, was recorded by the *New York Daily News*.

> A young father and mother said today they followed "God's will" in refusing a blood transfusion on religious grounds while their 9-day-old baby died.
>
> A doctor stood by, anxiously hoping the parents would change their mind. Authorities also sought to take the baby away from the parents by court order. But they were too late.
>
> The father, Thomas Grzyb, 20, said: "It was God's will. I would not have the child come back to life if it was against God's will. If I am called a murderer, that is God's will.
>
> "We want more children. But if such a thing happens again

and the child dies, that will be God's way, too." Grzyb said, "I will not interfere with God's will."

His wife, Barbara, 18, sobbed, "My baby, my baby," over and over. But she agreed with her husband. Both are members of Jehovah's Witnesses and said they followed biblical teachings that blood must not be used as food.

One more example of the stubborn resistance bordering on fanaticism which Jehovah's Witnesses display on the issue of blood transfusion is found in an article entitled, "Arrest 'Witnesses,' Give Woman Blood," in the *New York Daily News* of April 27, 1952. We quote the news item here in its entirety.

> Odessa, Tex., April 27 (U.P.)—The father and two brothers of a critically injured woman were arrested today when they tried to prevent a doctor from giving her a blood tranfusion considered necessary to save her life.
>
> Marie Oliff, 20, was given the blood as the three men were removed from the hospital room where she had lain unconscious for a week.
>
> The girl suffered a compound skull fracture, a fractured pelvis and fractures of both legs in an automobile collision, and her physician said she might die if she did not receive a transfusion immediately.
>
> Her father and brothers had stood guard at her room and said they would resort to force if anyone tried to give her blood. Members of the Jehovah's Witnesses religious sect, they claimed the Bible forbids transfusions.
>
> Miss Oliff regained consciousness briefly today and physicians decided to ask her if she would over-rule her family.
>
> First they asked if she was a member of Jehovah's Witnesses. "No," she replied.
>
> "Do you want a transfusion, if one is necessary?" a doctor asked.
>
> "Yes," she said.
>
> Her brothers, John 27, and Ben, 23, of 124 Columbia Heights, Brooklyn, were in the room.
>
> "Tell them you're a member of the Jehovah's Witnesses and you don't want a blood transfusion," John told his sister several times.
>
> Her father, William Oliff, 54, a Mirland, Tex., trailer camp operator, told doctors: "You're trying to kill my girl."

Acting under a court order, the doctors called police, who ousted the three men from the hospital room.

"You can't treat us like this unless you arrest us," John said.

"All right," an officer replied. "All three of you are under arrest. You're charged with disturbing peace. Let's go to jail."

The three were arraigned before Justice of the Peace Jack Parker and held in $250 bond each.

Miss Oliff's divorced husband, Clyde Wright of Odessa, got an injunction Wednesday restraining the family from interfering with a transfusion.

Think soberly on this brief story for one moment if you will, and the horror of this Watchtower dogma cannot help but grip you. Here were a father and two brothers so devoted to what the Watchtower *says* the Bible teaches, that they were willing to sacrifice the life of their own flesh and blood on the Russellite altar of ignorance. Even Judge Rutherford with all his faults would shudder at this travesty upon reason and Scripture.

A final example of Russellite blindness, all too common among Jehovah's Witnesses is found in another case here reproduced from the *New York Mirror* of June 20, 1955.

Religious convictions bowed to an emergency court order Sunday and a frail, nine-day-old girl was rushed to an Englewood, N.J., hospital for a blood transfusion against which her parents had fought as "contrary to the law of God."

An emergency midnight court session, held in Palisades Police headquarters, ended in the issuance of an order placing Gail Bertinato in the custody of Bergen County's Welfare Department after three physicians warned that unless the transfusion were given quickly she would die.

HER PARENTS, Louis, 26, and Gloria, 24, of 336 Second St., Palisades Park, who had fought since Friday to prevent the transfusion, took their defeat without rancor and told newsmen: "Our objections are scriptural. We were only doing our Christian duty. We had no other choice. God's law is supreme over any man-made law; you just don't break the law of God."

Members of Jehovah's Witnesses, they told the court that they believe blood transfusions are against the teachings of the Bible.

Gail, born June 10 in Jersey City, fell ill Friday and was found to be suffering from an RH negative factor, which means that her red corpuscles are not produced rapidly enough to meet the

body's needs. Dr. C. T. Markert of Ridgefield Park told the
parents that their baby was critically ill and should have an
immediate transfusion.

BUT THE PARENTS balked. Markert notified police Chief Leon-
ard Cottrell, who conferred with Bergen County Prosecutor Guy
W. Calissi. Digging into his law books, Calissi came up with a
little-known statute under which children may be placed in the
county's custody in emergency cases.

He filed a complaint with Juvenile and Domestic Relations
Court Judge Martin J. Kole late Saturday night—and Kole, ordering an immediate hearing issued a show-cause order requiring
the parents to appear before him.

Cottrell drove to their home to make one more effort to persuade them to consent to the transfusion. When they refused,
he took them before Kole—and it was then that the three doctors
voiced an unanimous warning that without a transfusion Gail
could not live.

RUSHED TO THE hospital by Cottrell and juvenile authorities as
soon as the hearing was over, Gail was given an emergency transfusion at 2 a.m. Hospital spokesmen described the baby's condition later as "still critical, but showing improvement."

Her parents said they will visit her "as often as the doctor per-
mits us."

In spite of such developments as the *Mirror* reported, Jehovah's Witnesses continue their blissful ploddings, and play with
the lives of little children who are helpless to protect themselves.
The Watchtower further declares, "Blood transfusion is *not* Christ
like . . . and doing it in disobedience to God's commands could
cost one eternal life."[5] It was the Lord Jesus who said, "Whosoever shall offend one of these little ones that believe in me, it is
better for him that a millstone were hanged about his neck, and
he were cast into the sea" (Mk 9:42, KJV). The Witnesses would
therefore do well to remember these words when they tamper
with the lives of innocent children.

Following hard upon the heels of the fleeing "Religionists,"
of whom the late lamented Judge J. F. Rutherford once said,
"They shall go down in defeat biting the dust as they go,"[6] the
zealous Witnesses affirm that "transfusions are a violation of the
everlasting covenant."[7] Just which covenant they are referring to

remains a mystery, since the Bible speaks of no covenant even remotely connected with blood transfusions.

There are many verifiable facts about the gigantic life-saving accomplishments of blood transfusions. (See *Blood, Your Gift of Life,* a Red Cross publication, for documentation.) Jehovah's Witnesses can offer but pitiful unscriptural criticism of so great a life-giving charity. The Lord Jesus said, "Greater love hath no man than this, that a man lay down his life for his friends" (Jn 15:13, KJV). It must be plain that Christ understood suffering in others and healed its causes whenever He encountered it. How much more should those of us His servants be ever ready to alleviate the pain and suffering of others if it lies within our power. The Bible never speaks against transfusion in any form, only against "eating blood" in a sacrificial or dietary manner. While it is true that hepatitis, a potentially fatal disease, can come from infected plasma, whole blood, or needles, as the Watchtower often points out, this has nothing to do with what the Bible says on the subject and must not be allowed to cloud the issue.

Jesus said, "By their fruits ye shall know them" (Mt 7:20, KJV). If the Watchtower has so little regard for human life that for the sake of unscriptural dogmatism, it will sacrifice the lives of its members and their children on the altar of unreasoning blindness, then their yield is clearly corrupt fruit. "Jehovah of the Watchtower" is not Jehovah of the Bible, who loves His children and sent His Son to be our Saviour. The sooner all know that Russellism has perpetrated this fraud with no sound medical or scriptural basis, the quicker it will be recognized for what it is. Truly, this Watchtower dogma is a shallow and narrow perversion of God's Word, devised by those who will not worship Jehovah of the Bible, and who have never received His Son, Jesus Christ, as their Saviour from sin.

In closing this chapter on the increasing activity of the Jehovah's Witness propaganda, it appears vitally important to the authors to mention a steadily growing branch of the Russellite system seldom if ever recognized for what it really is. We speak of "The Dawn Bible Students Movement" and its well-advertised coast-to-coast radio program, "Frank and Ernest" (heard Sundays, over hundreds of stations). This comparatively small but potent voice of Russellite propaganda is the modern-day successor to the original Russellite propaganda movement which split with J. F. Rutherford shortly after Pastor Russell's death (1916).‡

This group (they have over 30,000 subscribers to their monthly, *The Dawn*) remains wholly true to Russell's teaching (unlike Jehovah's Witnesses who have deviated slightly on minor points) and still teach his "pyramid" system of date compilation for prophetic purposes. One of the authors made an extensive and thorough tour (expertly guided by a "Dawnite," as they are sometimes called) of the movement's headquarters in East Rutherford, New Jersey, and had many opportunities to study their whole theological system. We even interviewed Frank of the "Frank and Ernest" program. The Dawnites agree to all of Russell's attacks on organized religion, reject the deity of Christ, the Trinity as "pagan," hell as a medieval myth. They do, however, accept the resurrection as the only hope for mankind (a second chance), but Christ's resurrection in a physical form is vehemently denied by them. Along with Russell, they believe that "the man Jesus is dead, forever dead." The foreman of the Dawn printing press, who had known Russell and had been in the movement for over fifty years, denounced the Watchtower (as did all the staff members we met) as perverters of the Pastor's works, although they admitted the doctrinal similarity between their respective group and Jehovah's Witnesses. The late Pastor Russell's pictures were to be seen everywhere on the premises, a mute testimony to the personality appeal of a man whose weird theological doctrines continue to live on long after his life has ended. The Dawnites advertise widely, and over the "Frank and Ernest" broadcasts, distribute countless pamphlets filled with Russellite theology. Unlike the Jehovah's Witnesses, the Dawnites harbor no hatred for people of other religions. They offer Russell's paradise on earth to all in the full persuasion that if one does not believe now, he will afterward wake up in the resurrection, which is the "second chance" for a "person of good will" or a "footstep follower of Jesus." Annihilation of those who re-

‡The Layman's Home Missionary Movement is another descendant of the Russellite splinters. Its headquarters are in Philadelphia, Pa.

ject Jehovah's theocracy is a view shared by the Dawnites, who reject eternal retribution. Jehovah's Witnesses concur in this also. The Watchtower in recent years returned to the old Russellite teaching that the wicked dead will be resurrected, instead of the belief that they remain in their graves; and the "Pastors" doctrine of a second chance seems to be coming into favor once again.

In summing up the Dawn movement, in all fairness, we must comment that they are deeply sincere in their beliefs, but as the Scriptures reveal, *sincerely wrong*. They are to be regarded in a spirit of Christian love as we try to win them to Christ.

6

Jehovah's Witnesses vs. Christendom and Clergymen

ATTITUDES FOSTERED BY RELIGIONS tell a great deal more about the particular members than all the volumes of propaganda circulated by the group in question. When dealing with Jehovah's Witnesses, it is, therefore, more profitable to observe the fruits of their theories than to listen to their clever barrages of pseudo-biblical propaganda.

Since we began writing about this controversial cult, many Jehovah's Witnesses and erstwhile "do-gooders" have become upset with what they term the "intolerant attitude" displayed by the authors toward the Watchtower movement. We would not trouble ourselves ordinarily to answer their line of criticism, except that in this case, we have been grossly misunderstood and misrepresented by various members of the Watchtower. To clarify what our attitude is as opposed to theirs, we wish to present what we believe to be more than ample evidence that their views are far more intolerant of all faiths, not just ours, than we have ever dreamed of being toward theirs. We, therefore, submit this chapter toward clearing up this unfortunate misconception on the part of Jehovah's Witnesses and their sympathizers. The following documentary evidence is just a small portion of comprehensive data available on how the Witnesses verbally persecute all who challenge their theories. This evidence is included in the hope of showing the true nature of those who purport to be the only Witnesses of Jehovah God on earth.

In the history of cultism, many strange varieties have arisen which were noted for their antagonism to various religious de-

nominations and people. But in this field, few of them can compare with "Jehovah's Witnesses," who literally "make hate a
religion"[1] and denounce all denominations and, for that matter,
all Christendom in the name of witnessing for Jehovah-God. In
the December 1951 edition of *The Watchtower*, the Witnesses,
with their customary zeal, hurl vindictive and sarcastic accusations at all Christendom on the subject of "showing concern for
the poor." Not content with comparing Christian-inspired charity
drives with "demonism" in Africa, "religious superstition" in
India, and godless "Red religion" in Communism, the Witnesses
proceed to accuse Christendom of being responsible for the very
miseries its charity drives are calculated to correct.[2]

The following is a sample of their attitude: "And in Christendom, surprising as it may seem to some, the false religious teachings, creeds, traditions, and commands of men are both directly
and indirectly responsible for the physical and spiritual miseries
of the poor, notwithstanding Christendom's showy display of
charity."[3]

Since it never in the least disturbs the Watchtower to skip from
subject to subject irrespective of any connection, they are found
in the next breath condemning Christendom for actually being
responsible in a large part for the cause of World Wars I and II.
They say, "Had Christendom chosen to do so, she could easily
have prevented World Wars I and II."[4] No one could ever honestly believe that Christendom ever wanted to hinder the preven-
tion of either of the two previous world wars. But Jehovah's Witnesses are content to teach this obvious error, with little unified
resistance on the part of Christians in all denominations.

As far as Christendom's interest in the poor and needy is concerned, the Witnesses maintain, "Christendom's pretended interest in the poor is sheer hypocrisy."[5] One would think that
after so bold an attack on all Christendom, *The Watchtower*
would abate for a time, but this is not the case. Breathing hotly
on the necks of the fleeing hordes of "hellfire screeching clergymen," as the Witnesses describe their clerical opponents, they
next read into the twenty-second chapter of Ezekiel a ringing
condemnation of Christendom which they wrongfully apply to
all those outside of their fold. We quote their paraphrase in full

to show the type of theological slander not uncommon in Jehovah's Witnesses' many literary efforts.

- Her priests have done violence to my law, and have profaned my holy things: . . . Her princes in the midst thereof are like wolves ravening the prey, to shed blood, and to destroy souls, that they may get dishonest gain. And her prophets have daubed for them with untempered mortar, seeing false visions, and divining lies unto them, saying, Thus said the Lord Jehovah, when Jehovah hath not spoken. (And as a result:) The people of the land have used oppression, and exercised robbery; yea, they have vexed the poor and needy, and have oppressed the sojourner wrongfully (Eze 22:26-29, ASV).[6]

In even more violent tones, the Witnesses continue their indictment. "Oh wicked Christendom," booms *The Watchtower,* "Why have you forsaken God's clean worship? Why have you joined forces and become part of Satan's wicked organization that oppresses the people? Why have you failed to show concern for the poor as Jehovah commands?" (paraphrase of Is 58:6-7).[7] This type of illogical reasoning with no concern for statistical facts or figures characterizes the constant baiting tactics employed by the Witnesses. The question is, How long will Christendom stand by in silence and listen to such unfounded and untruthful accusations? In the same edition of the *Watchtower,* the writer of the article continues, "The little charitable help the poor get from Christendom is like the crumbs the beggar Lazarus picked up from the rich man's table while the dogs licked his ulcerous sores. Neither the crumbs nor the licking remedied the beggarly condition. Only Jehovah can effect a rescue. How comforting then for the dejected, downtrodden people of the earth to learn that there is one 'higher than the highest,' of Christendom's moguls."[8] Completely ignoring the tens of millions of dollars expended by Christendom's millions of people for the alleviation of suffering on the part of the poor and needy, Jehovah's Witnesses wantonly decry in effect that nobody is doing anything worthwhile but them— the only true servants of Jehovah-God. What a gigantic misrepresentation of facts; what a deplorable perversion of existing conditions and Christian efforts made by others.

The reader might ask, Do Jehovah's Witnesses really believe

that they are the only ones exerting a constructive charity effort in behalf of the poor? Surely you have misrepresented them. For the benefit of anyone naive enough to believe that the Witnesses are not dogmatic in this fabrication, we quote their own statement when, after condemning Christendom for her failure, they heap all the honor for aiding the poor upon their own "humble" heads when they write: "Yes, Jehovah the Almighty hears the cries of the half-dead ones, and hearing He answers their prayers and sends His 'Good Samaritans' to the rescue, even the *Witnesses* who are despised by Christendom,"[9] Such is the character of their self-righteousness that they actually believe themselves God's chief instruments for tending the needs of the poor.

Pastor Russell, their now well-concealed* founder, would be very proud of his Russellite followers, as would his erstwhile late successor, Judge J. F. Rutherford. These chief apostles of Russellism have taught their disciples well the arts of linguistic trickery and unflinching boldness, traits which always characterize the efforts of Jehovah's Witnesses.

To refute the error that little help is given to the poor and needy by Christendom, one need only scan the financial records of the various major denominations who yearly support countless hospitals, charities, orphanages, homes for the aged, and medical research projects. The truth of the whole matter is that Jehovah's Witnesses cannot afford to give Christendom credit for doing anything well, as it would be an admission of their failure to properly supervise the theocratic kingdom, since Christendom would be doing good while rejecting the Witnesses' testimony.

We challenge Jehovah's Witnesses to make public their contribution figures where charity is concerned, so that if they must condemn others, let them at least show some evidence for it and in so doing, demonstrate their benevolence by listing their own distribution of assets to the poor and needy whom we are represented as abusing. Either the Witnesses produce such facts or they must remain silent concerning a matter which they obviously know very little about where Christendom is concerned. The Watchtower allowed Marley Cole, a Southern newspaper

---

*That is his unsavory past, and theological importance to the movement. They mention him only when necessary and then in the briefest terms.

reporter, to publish these figures in his book, *Jehovah's Witnesses—The New World Society*. In this pro-Russellite book, Cole neglects to point out that the contributions went almost exclusively to fellow Witnesses, not to the needy in general, except where these gifts might aid the conversion of the needy to Jehovah's Witnesses.

Continuing on with the Watchtower's attitude of "tolerance," an interesting article appears in the October 1, 1952, issue of *The Watchtower*, entitled "Jehovah a Strong Refuge Today." In this enlightening article, the Witnesses write concerning their feelings toward "enemies of God" (Christendom):

> Haters of God and His people [Jehovah's Witnesses], etc., are to be hated, but this does not mean that we will take any opportunity of bringing physical hurt to them in a spirit of malice or spite, for both malice and spite belong to the Devil, whereas pure hatred does not. We must hate in the truest sense, which is to regard with extreme and active aversion, to consider as loathsome, odius, filthy, to detest. Surely any haters of God are not fit to live on his beautiful earth. The earth will be rid of the wicked and we shall not need to lift a finger to cause physical harm to come to them, for God will attend to that, but we must have a proper perspective of these enemies. His name signifies recompense to the enemies.
>
> Jehovah's enemies are recognized by their intense dislike for his people and the work these are doing. For they would break it down and have all of Jehovah's Witnesses sentenced to jail or concentration camps if they could. Not because they have anything against the witnesses personally, but on account of their work. They publish blasphemous lies and reproach the holy name Jehovah. Do we not hate those who hate God? We cannot love those hateful enemies, for they are fit only for destruction. We utter the prayer of the psalmist: "How long, O God, shall the adversary reproach? Shall the enemy blaspheme thy name forever? Why drawest thou back thy hand, even thy right hand? Pluck it out of thy bosom and consume them" (Ps. 74:10, 11, A.S.V.). We pray with intensity and cry out this prayer for Jehovah to delay no longer, and plead that his anger be made manifest. . . . O Jehovah God of hosts, . . . be not merciful to any wicked transgressors. . . . Consume them in wrath, consume them, so that they shall be no more: . . . (Ps. 59:4-6, 11-13,

A. S. V.). These are the true sentiments, desires and prayers of
the righteous ones today. Are they yours? . . . How we despise
the workers of iniquity, and those who would tear down God's
organization! . . . O Jehovah. Let them be put to shame and
dismayed for ever; yea, let them be confounded and perish; that
they may know that thou alone, whose name is Jehovah, art the
Most High over all the earth (Ps. 83:9-18, A. S. V.).[10]

After clearly showing their feelings toward all those who, they
say, "hate Jehovah and His people," the Witnesses go on further
in the same article to link Christendom universal, both Protestant
and Catholic, with these unbelievable accusations. In the same
issue, they apply the account of the wickedness of Moab, who
persecuted the children of Israel, to Christendom, and accuse
Christendom of being a hater of Jehovah! The following are their
own words, so none can doubt.

> The near neighbors of Judah . . . had been the opposers of the
> Israelites right from the time when refusal was given by them
> to supply provisions to Israel as they journeyed to the promised
> land. Moab hired Balaam to curse Israel. (See also Numbers
> 22; 23; 24; 25:1-5 and Deuteronomy 23:3) They had much
> contempt for Jehovah's people, and prided themselves on their
> own "lofty city," her counterpart today being that rich, lofty
> city, the mighty religious organization standing for the whole of
> Satan's organization. The modern-day Moabites are the profess-
> ing Christians, whose words and actions are as far removed from
> Christianity and pure worship of Jehovah as Moab was removed
> from true worship and the covenant of Jehovah. Jehovah had
> warned Moab of his proposed punishment for her iniquity and
> opposition.
>
> The modern-day Moabites have opposed Jehovah's Witnesses
> with a hatred not born of righteousness, but from the Devil and
> against all righteousness. Their hatred for God's true people in-
> creases as they see us upon the very plain evidence of Jehovah's
> favor and the obvious disfavor they themselves are in. They put
> forth every effort to prevent the people of good will from enter-
> ing the new world. They are richer than Jehovah's Witnesses in
> material things and with it they have much pride and arrogance.
>
> The modern-day Moabites will be brought low, for Jehovah
> has completely finished with them. Hear just a part of the pun-
> ishment: "For in this mountain will the hand of Jehovah rest;

and Moab shall be trodden down in his place, even as straw is trodden down in the water of the dunghill. And he shall spread forth his hands in the midst thereof, as he that swimmeth spreadeth forth his hands to swim; but Jehovah will lay low his pride together with the craft of his hands." It is a sure thing that one cannot have much pride left when one is being pressed down into a manure pile, showing the utter contempt Jehovah has for modern-day Moab, keeping her wallowing in the mire of shame. "For thou has made of a city a heap, of a fortified city a ruin, a palace of strangers to be no city; it shall never be built." "For he hath brought down them that dwell on high, the lofty city: he layeth it low, he layeth it low even to the ground; he bringeth it even to the dust. The foot shall tread it down; even the feet of the poor, and the steps of the needy" (Isa. 25:2, 10, 11; 26:5, 6, A. S. V.).

When this happens, what a tremendous change will take place! The tables will be turned! Brought down will be the lofty from dwelling on high as the great, high, influential ones of this world, to the lowest possible place imaginable, so low and degraded that it can only be compared to being trampled underfoot by the poor like straw on a manure heap. Christendom's lofty looks, boastful words, bragging tongue, her superior attitude toward the holy Word of God, her trust in idols and men and riches, such as belong to this world, will not provide her with security or any safety from Jehovah's storm and blast. They have no defense and are disgraced.

Christendom's defenses are of no value, but Jehovah's witnesses have a "strong city," and this is something to sing about. There are millions who want a safe place and are in need of security. Let them know we have a "strong city"! "Thou shalt call thy walls Salvation, and thy gates Praise" (Isa. 60:18, A. S. V.). Only God's kingdom offers such protection and salvation, for inside the city one is then safe. Those desiring salvation must make for God's organization, and find entrance into it and remain there permanently.[11]

Such are the attitudes and views on tolerance subscribed to by the Jehovah's Witnesses. Notice they say, "Both malice and spite belong to the Devil, whereas 'pure hatred' does not."[12] On pages 336, 438, 698 of Webster's Encyclopedic Dictionary, the terms *hate, malice,* and *spite* are defined exhaustively but all amount to about the same thing, that is, a spirit of malevolence or ill will toward others. However, nowhere is *pure hate* (p. 500) differentiated from plain old-fashioned hatred as the Witnesses try to make it appear. To the authors, it seems that one can hardly desire to win a soul to salvation through faith in the loving Christ of Calvary when the heart is filled with "pure hatred" for the sinner.

Jehovah's Witnesses, of course, claim that they do not hate the sinner, only the enemies of Jehovah-God and His people. Nevertheless, the Bible declares that all sinners are at enmity with God (Ro 8:7) or, in our modern sense, showing ill will, hostility, or hatred toward Him. Hence, Jehovah's Witnesses find no ground for hatred since, if their contention is true, they must hate everyone, for all men are sinners (Ro 3:23). There is not the slightest doubt in the minds of the authors that Jehovah's Witnesses hate whoever opposes their theocracy.

In the words of Stanley High, "Jehovah's Witnesses hate everybody and try to make it mutual." With Mr. High's words we heartily concur. Jehovah's Witnesses disseminate this kind of propaganda from dawn till dusk, and Christendom has failed to answer adequately their accusations. We have been accused of dishonoring Jehovah-God, misrepresenting His Word, exalting His Son over Him, hating and persecuting His Witnesses, failing to care for the poor and needy, and in general rejecting "the truth" of His theocratic organization, represented by the Watchtower Bible and Tract Society. As a result of these alleged crimes against God and nature, Christendom and her clergy have been branded "enemies of God" and "instruments of the devil" fit only for the dung heap of "everlasting destruction." With Jehovah's Witnesses, it is easy to see the quality of mercy is never strained and Christian love is altogether obscured by the thunderings of the Russell-Rutherford theology. Such is the destiny of all those who dare criticize the visible theocracy. These outraged roars of hate against Christendom and the clergy by Jehovah's Witnesses is a far cry from their own *New World Translation's* rendering of the great command to love all, as found in the gospels of Matthew and Luke.

The Lord Jesus said in answer to the hate mongers of His day, "You heard that it was said, 'You must love your neighbor and hate your enemy.' However, I say to you, 'Continue to love your enemies, and to pray for those persecuting you, that you may prove yourself sons of your father who is in the heavens'" (Mt 5:43-45, NWT).

Not only this, but the Lord expressly repeated His injunction as Luke records it in the sixth chapter of his gospel, "But I say to you who are listening, 'continue to love your enemies, to do good to those hating you, to bless those cursing you, to pray for those who do you injury'" (Lk 6:27-28, NWT).

Now if we were the malicious haters and enemies of Jehovah's Witnesses, which we are not, according to their own translation, they should love us, but *The Watchtower* says we are "odious, loathsome, and filthy," and to be avoided because we are "haters of God" since we reject their Russellite theology.

This attitude of hatred on the Witnesses' part is one of their pet doctrines of long standing. As far back as 1928, the then Supreme Potentate of Russellite Wisdom, Judge J. F. Rutherford, said concerning Christendom and the clergy:

> God has been grossly misrepresented by the clergy. If this statement is true [and he later declares that it *is* true], then that alone is proof conclusive that the clergy do not in fact represent God and Christ but do represent God's enemy, the Devil. . . . Torture is repulsive even to the imperfect men. Only a selfish, hard, cruel, and wicked one could inflict conscious eternal torment upon another. . . . The theory of eternal torment in Hell is the outgrowth of . . . Satanic lie. These doctrines originated with the Devil. They have long been taught by his representatives. . . . The clergy have been his instruments freely used to instill these false doctrines into the minds of men. Whether the clergy have willingly done so or not does not alter the fact. . . . The clergy have at all times posed as the representatives of God on earth. Satan overreached the minds of these clergymen and injected into their minds doctrines . . . which . . . the clergy have taught the people concerning Jesus and His sacrifice. These doctrines have brought great confusion.[13]

The Judge went even further in his hate campaign when he wrote concerning the doctrine of the Trinity as taught by Christendom's clergy.

The clergy have even held to this senseless, God dishonoring doctrine. . . . If you ask a clergyman what is meant by the Trinity, he says: "That is a mystery." He does not know, and no one else knows, because it is false. . . . They (the clergy) are willingly or unwillingly the instruments in the hands of Satan, the Devil, who has used them to blind the minds of the people, to prevent the people from understanding God's great plan of salvation and reconciliation.[14]

The Watchtower, or Jehovah's Witnesses, have never repudiated Rutherford's declarations, rather they have affirmed them, and in places have even lifted his writings word for word to put in new books. Since basically the theology never changes from Russell and Rutherford through Knorr, they can make use of the Judge's material whenever they need some peppery seasoning agent in *The Watchtower*.

Reviewing the mass of indictments and undocumented charges against Christendom and the clergy, the Christian cannot help but be shocked at the accusations hurled helter-skelter by the Witnesses. If they were a small group, we might dismiss their unfounded dogmas and vilifications as plain ignorance, love their souls, hate their sins, and pray for their salvation. However, they are a large and rapidly growing group and apparently despise the prayers of those outside the theocracy and treat with aloof disdain any attempt to criticize their beliefs. They triumphantly cry, "We have the truth!" and refuse all biblical wisdom unless it is approved by their Society. Not only this, but they attack, without remorse or consideration, the beliefs of Christendom, the clergy, and all others with arrogance indescribable for its lack of tact, kindness, or Christian love. We cannot ignore such uncharitable slander, lest our silence be construed as an admission of guilt. We must "take arms against this sea of troubles and by opposing end them" to the best of our Christian ability, and in a spirit of true Christian love. We do not hate Jehovah's Witnesses nor have we ever abused them physically, emotionally, or verbally. Our one desire is to stanch their flow of misrepresentation where Christendom and the clergy are concerned and compel them by the sheer force of Christian love, tolerance, and prayer, to meet with us upon the level plane of scriptural truth, independent of Russellite theology, and present or defend their views. We feel we have been more than fair in this respect, much more so than they, and to our critics we earnestly say: Compare the record and see who has been misrepresenting whom—Jehovah's Witnesses or the clergy.

7

Jehovah's Witnesses vs. the Scriptures, Reason, and the Trinity

EVERY MAJOR CULT and non-Christian religion which seeks to deride orthodox theology continually attacks the doctrine of the Trinity. Jehovah's Witnesses (the Russellites of today) are the most vehement in this endeavor, and because they couch their clever misuse of terminology in scriptural contexts, they are also the most dangerous. This chapter is included therefore to present typical examples of Watchtower propaganda.

Such a typical example is found in the January 1, 1953, edition of *The Watchtower*, wherein the ever zealous disciples of Pastor Russell continue their tirade against the Trinity doctrine. This article, in particular, gives a clear picture of Jehovah's Witnesses' confused concept of biblical theology as well as their standard for measuring the validity of divine revelation.

Throughout the whole length and breadth of the Watchtower's turbulent history, one "criterion" has been used in every era to measure the credibility of any biblical doctrine. This "criterion" is *reason*. During the era of Pastor Russell and right through until today, *reason* has always been "the great god" before whom all followers of the Millennial Dawn (the original name of Jehovah's Witnesses) movement bow with unmatched reverence. In fact, the "great paraphraser," as Russell was once dubbed, even went so far as to claim that reason (the ability to think and draw conclusions) opened up to the intellect of man the very character of God Himself! Think of it! According to the pastor, God's nature is actually openly accessible to our feeble and erring reasoning powers. In the first volume of the "Millennial Dawn" series (later changed to *Studies in the Scriptures*), Pastor Russell

116

makes God subject to our powers of reasoning. Wrote the pastor: "Let us examine the character of the writings claimed as inspired, (The Bible) *to see whether their teachings* correspond with the character we have reasonably imputed to God."[1] For Russell, man's understanding of God's character lies, not in God's revelation of Himself to be taken by faith, but in our ability to reason out that character, subject to the laws of our reasoning processes. Russell obviously never considered Jehovah's Word as recorded in the fifty-fifth chapter of Isaiah the prophet, which discourse clearly negates man's powers of reasoning in relation to the divine character and nature of his Creator.

"For my thoughts are not your thoughts, neither are your ways my ways, saith the LORD. For as the heavens are higher than the earth, so are my ways higher than your ways, and my thoughts than your thoughts" (Is 55:8-9, KJV). By this statement, God certainly did not say reason and thought should be abandoned in the process of inquiry, but merely that no one can know the mind, nature, or thoughts of God in all their fullness, seeing that man is finite and He is infinite. The term *reason* and derivatives of it (*reasonable, reasoning, reasoned,* etc.) are used eighty-eight times in the English Bible, and only *once* in all these usages (Is 1:18) does God address man. Jehovah's Witnesses maintain that since God said, "Come now, and let us reason together" that He therefore gave reason a high place, even using it Himself to commune with His creatures. While this is true, it is only so in a limited sense at best. God never said, "Reason out the construction of My spiritual substance and nature," or, "Limit My character to your reasoning powers." Nevertheless, Jehovah's Witnesses, by making Christ (Logos, Jn 1:1) "a god" or a "mighty god," but not "Jehovah-God," have done just these things. In the reference quoted above (Is 1:18), Jehovah showed man the way of salvation and invited him to be redeemed from sin. God never invited him to explore His deity or probe into His mind. The apostle Paul says, "For who hath known the mind of the Lord? or who hath been his counsellor? Or who hath first given to him, and it shall be recompensed unto him again? For of him, and through him, and to him, are all things: to whom be glory for ever" (Ro 11:34-36, KJV).

But now, let us examine this typical propaganda from *The Watchtower's* arsenal and see if they really do follow Pastor Russell and his theory of reason. In this article, "The Scriptures, Reason, and the Trinity," referred to earlier in the chapter, the Witnesses constantly appeal to *reason* as the standard for determining what God thinks. The following are quotations which we believe illustrate this point beyond doubt.

> To hold that Jehovah God the Father and Christ Jesus His Son are co-eternal is to fly in the face of reason.[2]

Notice that reason is used as the "yardstick" to determine the validity of a scriptural doctrine.

> Jehovah God says: "Come now, and let us reason together" (Isaiah 1:18). The advocates of the Trinity admit that it is not subject to *reason** or logic, and so they resort to terming it a "mystery." *But the Bible contains no divine mysteries.* It contains "sacred secrets." Every use of the word "mystery" and "mysteries" in the *King James Version* comes from the same Greek root word meaning "to shut the mouth," that is to keep secret. *There is a vast difference between a secret and a mystery. A secret is merely that which has not been made known, but a mystery is that which cannot be understood.*[3]

Once again, the reader must pay close attention to the Witnesses' favorite game of term-switching. The Watchtower makes a clever distinction between the term *mystery* and the term *secret* and declares that "the Bible contains no divine mysteries." It is affirmed that "a secret is merely that which has not been made known, but a mystery is that which cannot be understood." In view of the seriousness of this Watchtower exercise in semantic trickery, we feel obliged to destroy their *manufactured* distinction between *secret* and *mystery,* by the simple process of consulting the latest dictionary available. On page 1044 of the *Webster's New Collegiate Dictionary* (1973), *secret* is defined as, "Something kept hidden or unexplained: MYSTERY." The word *mystery* is given in small capitals to indicate that it is synonymous with the entry word, *secret.* Surely this is proof conclusive that the Bible contains "divine mysteries" as far as the meaning of term is understood. It must also be equally apparent that Jeho-

*Emphasis added.

vah's Witnesses obviously have no ground for rejecting the word *mystery* where either the Bible or the dictionary are concerned. We fail to note any "vast difference" between the two words, and so does the dictionary. The truth is that the Watchtower rejects the Trinity doctrine and other cardinal doctrines of historic Christianity, not because they are mysterious, but because Jehovah's Witnesses are determined to reduce Jesus, the Son of God, to a creature or "a second god," all biblical evidence notwithstanding. They still follow in Pastor Russell's footsteps, and one needs no dictionary to substantiate that.

"Jehovah God by His Word furnishes us with ample *reasons* and logical bases for all regarding which he expects us to exercise faith. . . . We can make sure of what is right *only* by a process of *reasoning* on God's Word."[4]

Here indeed is a prime example of what Jehovah's Witnesses continually represent as sound thinking. They cannot produce even one shred of evidence to bolster up their unscriptural claim that God always gives us reasons for those things in which He wants us to "exercise faith." Biblical students (even "International"† ones) really grasp at theological straws when they attempt to prove so dogmatic and inconclusive a statement. A moment of reflection on the Scriptures will show, we believe, that this attempt to overemphasize *reason* is a false one.

First, does God give us a reason for creating Satan, the author of sin? Is such a reason found in the Scripture? It is not, and yet we must believe that he exists, that he opposes God, and that all references in the Scripture to Satan are authoritative. God demands that we exercise faith in their objective truth, yet He *never* gives us a reason for it.

Second, does God anywhere give to man a fathomable *reason* for choosing one person to salvation and rejecting another to eternal punishment? No. Never in the Scripture does He give a "reasonable" answer to this power of choice He exercises. As a matter of fact, He even politely tells us to mind our own business, as recorded in the ninth chapter of Romans: "I will have mercy on whom I will have mercy, and I will have compassion on whom I will have compassion" (KJV). So it depends not upon man's

†International Bible Students is one of the other names for Russellites.

will or exertion, but upon God's mercy. He has mercy upon whomever He wills, and He hardens the heart of whomever He wills, "O man, who art thou that repliest against God? Shall the thing formed say to him that formed it, Why hast thou made me thus? Hath not the potter power over the clay, of the same lump to make one vessel unto honour, and another unto dishonour?" (9:20-21, KJV). *All* this God requires us to believe on faith—no human reasons needed.

Third, does God anywhere give man a reason for children being born deaf, blind, crippled, or diseased? Does He anywhere clearly give understandable reasons for the suffering of circumstantially innocent people during wartime, for the death of an only son, or for untold human misery and suffering for apparently no good reasons? But through it all, God asks us to believe that these seemingly indescribable evils will ultimately work out His divine plan, and He asks us at times to believe in Him *against reason* and with the eyes of faith.

Much more could be said along the same lines, but enough has been shown to refute adequately the contention of Jehovah's Witnesses that God *always* gives us "reasons and logical bases" for all regarding which He expects us to exercise faith.

Let us also remember the falsity of their other claim in the same paragraph: "We can make sure of what is right only by a process of reasoning on God's Word."[5] This is such a trivial contention that it demands little effort for complete refutation. Jesus said, "Without me ye can do nothing" (Jn 15:5, KJV); and, "The Comforter, which is the Holy Ghost, whom the Father will send in my name, he shall teach you all things, and bring all things to your remembrance, whatsoever I have said unto you" (Jn 14:26, KJV). Now if "only by a process of reasoning on God's Word we can make sure of what is right," as Jehovah's Witnesses contend, then Jesus and they are at direct variance, for they do not have the guidance of the Holy Spirit, since they deny His person and deity. In a controversy of this nature, we prefer God and His Word to the Watchtower's jumbled Russellism.

Fourth, "God, through His Word, appeals to our reason. The Trinity doctrine is a negation of both the Scriptures and reason."[6] Concluding Jehovah's Witnesses use and abuse of the term *rea-*

son and its functions, we should like to call attention to the above sentences. Like so many other of the Watchtower's clever examples of phraseology, this statement contains a mixture of truth and error, with just enough of the former to make good sense, and just enough of the latter to confuse the reader. It is unquestionably true that God through His Word appeals to our reason; were it not so, we could not understand His desires. But by the same token, God does not invite our inquiry into His nature or character. Jehovah's Witnesses, however, if their views are rightly understood, assume that human *reason* is capable of doing just that.

The Watchtower has never failed to echo the old Arian heresy from the dawn of its existence via Pastor Russell, since it is upon this one long-exploded theological myth that the entire Jehovah's Witness movement unsteadily rests. Jehovah's Witnesses know beyond doubt that if Jesus is Jehovah-God, then every one of them is going to a flaming hereafter; and hell they fear above all else. This no doubt explains a great deal of their antagonism to the doctrines of the Trinity and hell. The Witnesses, it must be remembered, consistently berate the Trinity doctrine as "of the devil," and never tire proclaiming that "the Bible hell is the grave." The thought of being punished in unquenchable fire for their disobedience to God is probably the strongest bond that binds the Watchtower's flimsy covers together.

Let us further pursue the Watchtower's logic. In *The Watchtower's* various articles, two other terms are repeated constantly by Jehovah's Witnesses. These terms are *equal* and *coeternal.* The terms are used some six times in this particular article, and each time it is denied that Jesus Christ is either equal to or co-eternal with God His Father. Says *The Watchtower*:

> We see God in heaven as the Superior One . . . We see his Son on earth expressing delight to do his Father's will; clearly two separate and distinct personalities and *not* at all equal. Nothing here (Matthew 28:18-20) to indicate that it (The Holy Spirit) is a person, let alone that it is equal with Jehovah God [p. 21]. The very fact that the Son received his life from the Father proves that *he could not be co-eternal* with him. (John 1:18; 6:57) . . . Nor can it be argued that God was superior to

Jesus only because of Jesus' then being a human, for *Paul makes clear that Christ Jesus in his prehuman form was not equal with his father.* Philippians 2:1-11 (N.W.T.) he counsels Christians not to be motivated by egotism but to have lowliness of mind, even as Christ Jesus had, who, although existing in God's form before coming to earth, was not *ambitious* to become equal with his Father [p. 22] . . . Jesus did not claim to be *The God,* but *only* God's Son. That Jesus is inferior to his Father, is also apparent . . . etc. [p. 23] . . . The 'Holy Ghost' or Holy Spirit is God's active force . . . There is no basis for concluding that the Holy Spirit is a Person . . . Yes, the Trinity finds its origin in the pagan concept of a multiplicity, plurality, or pantheon of Gods. The law Jehovah God gave to the Jews stated diametrically the opposite. 'Jehovah our God is *one* Jehovah' (Deuteronomy 6:4).[7]

Let us briefly examine these statements of Jehovah's Witnesses and see if they have any rational content where the Bible is concerned. The Watchtower maintains that Christ and His Father are "not at all equal," which has been their boldest insult to Christianity since Russell and Rutherford concocted and promoted the whole Watchtower theology. This erroneous teaching where Christ's true deity is concerned has gladdened the hearts of unbelievers, who find it easier to mock the Trinity than to trust God's Word and His Son. Concerning His relationship with the Father, the apostle John in the fifth chapter of his gospel, the eighteenth verse, when speaking of Jesus and the Jews said, "Therefore the Jews sought the more to kill him, because he not only had broken the sabbath, but said also God was his Father, making himself equal with God" (KJV). The Greek word for equal is *ison,* which according to Thayer's *Greek Lexicon,* means "equal in quality as in quantity, to claim for one's self the *Nature,* rank, authority, which belong to God."[8] Dr. Thayer, Jehovah's Witnesses might take notice, was a Unitarian who denied Christ's deity even as they themselves do; yet, being honest, he gave the true meaning of the biblical terms, even though they contradicted his views. Thus God's Word directly contradicts Jehovah's Witnesses, and this they dare not deny.

The Watchtower further contends that since Christ received life from His Father—"I live by the Father" (Jn 6:57, KJV)—He could not be coeternal with Him. At first glance this seems plausible, especially when coupled with John 5:26: "As the Father hath life in himself, so hath he given to the Son to have life in himself" (KJV). Taking this text in its context, we readily see that it cannot mean that Christ derived "eternal existence" from the Father. John 1:1 bears witness that "the Word was God;" therefore eternity was inherent in His makeup by nature. The logical conclusion must be that the indwelling "life" of "God the Word" entered time in the form of "the Son of man," and by this operation, the Father through the agency of the Holy Spirit, gave the "Son of man" to have "life in Himself," the same life that was eternally His as the eternal Word. But it takes more than a glance to support this garbled Watchtower polytheism, as we shall soon see. Unwittingly, Jehovah's Witnesses answer their own scriptural double-talk when they quote Philippians 2:5-11 on page 22 of their article. In this passage of Scripture, Paul claims full deity for Christ and maintains that in His preincarnate life, He "existed in a form of God" and "thought it not something to be grasped at to be *equal* with God, but took upon himself the *form* of a servant and was made in the likeness of men" (KJV). The term *equal* here is another form of *ison*, namely *isa*, which again denotes *absolute sameness* of *nature*, thus confirming Christ's true deity. Further, this context reveals beyond reasonable doubt that *all* reference to Christ's being subject to His Father (Jn 5:26; 6:57) pertain to His earthly existence, during which "he emptied himself" to become as one of us. This in no way affected His true deity or unity with the Father, for Jesus claimed Jehovahistic identity (Jn 8:58) when He announced Himself to the unbelieving Jews as the "I AM" of Exodus 3:14. Twice, then, in the same terms, Jehovah's Witnesses deny what the Scriptures specifically testify, that Christ *is equal* with God in essence, character, and nature, which truths the Watchtower can never change. We should also like to call attention to an extremely bold example of misquoting so commonly found in Watchtower propaganda. The Russellite oracle declares, *"Paul makes clear that Christ Jesus in his prehuman form was not equal to his father. In Philippians 2:1-11 (NWT) he counsels Christians not to be motivated by egotism but to have lowliness of mind even as Christ Jesus had, who, although existing in God's form before* coming to earth *was not ambitious to become equal with his Father.*"⁹

Now as far as the original Greek text of Philippians 2:1-11 is concerned, this is an absurd and plainly dishonest statement. Paul never even mentions Christ's being ambitious to attain anything at all or even His lack of ambition, since no Greek term there can be translated "ambition." Jehovah's Witnesses themselves do not use the word *ambition* in their own *New World Translation,* nor does any other translator that we know of. Despite this, however, they introduce the term which clouds the real meaning of the Greek terms. Further than this, and worse, the Watchtower plainly attempts to use Paul's declaration of Christ's deity as a means of confusing the issue. They maintain that Paul here taught that Jesus was inferior in nature to His Father, when in reality, Paul's entire system of theology is just the opposite. If we are to believe the Greek text, Paul declares that Jesus did *not* consider equality with God something "to be grasped after, or robbed" (*arpazo,* Greek) since He previously existed as the eternal Word of God (Jn 1:1) prior to His incarnation (Jn 1:14), and as such shared the Father's prerogatives and attributes. Hence, He had no desire to strive for what was His by nature and inheritance. Paul elsewhere calls Christ "all the fullness of the Deity in the flesh" (Col 2:9), "the great God and our Saviour" (Titus 2:13, KJV), and "God" (Heb 1:3, 8). These are just a few of the references; there are at least twenty-five more which could be cited from his writings and over seventy-five from the balance of the New Testament. Contrary to the Watchtower, then, Paul never wrote their Russellite interpretational paraphrase, since even the Greek text bears witness against them.

Though it is rudimentary to any study of the Bible, the personality and deity of the Holy Spirit must be defended constantly also against the attacks of the Watchtower.

The Watchtower denies His personality and deity, but the following references, a few of the many in Scripture, refute their stand completely:

1. Acts 5:3-4. In verse 3, Peter accuses Ananias of lying *to* the Holy Spirit; and in verse 4, he declares that Ananias had lied to

God, thus equating the Holy Spirit with the Godhead, an equation hard for the Watchtower to explain, much less to deny. Also, who else but a person can be lied to?

2. Acts 13:2, 4. In the context, the Holy Spirit speaks and sends, as He does in 21:10-11, where He prophesies Paul's imprisonment. Only a personality can do these things, *not* "an invisible active force," as the Jehovah's Witnesses describe Him.

3. Such references as John 14:16-17, 26; and 16:7-14 need no comment. *He* is a divine person, and He is God (Gen 1:2).

4. Acts 20:23. The Holy Spirit testifies, something only a person can do (Ro 8:16, 26; 1 Jn 5:6).

5. Acts 10:28; 16:6; and 1 Corinthians 2:13. The Spirit reasons, forbids, and teaches.

Jehovah's Witnesses sum up their blast at the Trinity doctrine by informing us that John 1:1 should be rendered, "In the beginning was the Word and the Word was with God and the Word was *a god.*" This is another example of the depths to which the Watchtower will descend to make Jesus "a second god" and thus introduce polytheism into Christianity. Needless to say, no recognized translators in the history of Greek exegesis have ever sanctioned such a grammatical travesty as the Watchtower translation, and the Watchtower translators know it. Such a rendition is an indication of markedly inferior scholarship and finds no basis whatsoever in New Testament Greek grammar. Both James Moffat and Edgar Goodspeed, liberal translators, render John 1:1: "the Word was Divine"; but Mantey translates it, "the Word was Deity," or God, as does every acknowledged authority. Moffat and Goodspeed, also admit it teaches the full and *equal* deity of Jesus Christ, something Jehovah's Witnesses vehemently deny. Beyond doubt, the Watchtower of Jehovah's Witnesses presents a strange dilemma, "ever learning, and never able to come to a knowledge of the truth." The Russellite movements (there are other small branches) all cry loudly the old Jewish Scripture, "Hear, O Israel, the Lord our God is *one* Lord" (or, "The Lord is One"), and attempt to use it against the doctrine of the Trinity. But once again, language betrays the shallowness of their resources. The term *ECHOD*, "one" in Hebrew, does *not* denote *absolute* unity in many places throughout the Old Testament, and often it

definitely denotes *composite unity*, which argues for the Trinity
of the Deity (Jehovah). In Genesis 2:24, the Lord tells us that
"a man leaves his father and his mother and cleaves to his wife,
and they become one flesh" (*BOSOR ECHOD*, Hebrew). Certainly this does not mean that in marriage a man and his wife
become one *person*, but that they become *one* in the unity of
their substance and are considered as *one* in the eyes of God.
Please note, this is true unity; yet *not solitary*, but *composite*
unity. Let us further consider composite unity. Moses sent
twelve spies into Canaan (Num 13), and when they returned
they brought with them a great cluster of grapes (*ESCHOL
ECHOD*, Hebrew). Now since there were hundreds of grapes
on this one stem, it could hardly be absolute or solitary unity, yet
again *ECHOD* (one) is used to describe the cluster. This shows
that the grapes were considered one, in the sense of their being of
the same origin; hence, *composite unity* is again demonstrated.
Jehovah's Witnesses continually ask, If Jesus when on the cross
was truly an incarnation of Jehovah, then who was in heaven?
This is a logical question to which the eighteenth chapter of
Genesis gives fourteen answers, each reaffirming the other. As
recorded in the eighteenth chapter of Genesis, Abraham had
three visitors, two of them were later called angels (Gen 19:1),
but the third he addressed as "Jehovah God," *fourteen times!*
Abraham's third visitor stayed and conversed with him and then
departed, saying, concerning Sodom, "I will go down and see
whether they have done altogether according to the outcry which
has come to me, and if not, I will know" (18:21). And so, "The
Lord went his way, when he had finished speaking to Abraham,
and Abraham returned to his place" (v. 33). Now if John is to be
believed without question, and Jehovah's Witnesses agree that he
must be, then "No man hath seen God [the Father] at any time;
the only begotten Son [Jesus Christ] which is in the bosom of the
Father, he hath declared him" (Jn 1:18, KJV). To further confuse the Witnesses' peculiar view of God as a *solitary unit*, Jesus
Himself said concerning His Father, "You have not at any time
either heard his voice *or* seen his form . . . for God is Spirit, and
they that worship him must worship him in Spirit and in truth"
(Jn 5:37; 4:24). Now then, here is the evidence. Moses declares

that God spoke face to face with Abraham (Gen 18:1), and Jesus and John, say, "No man hath seen God at any time." But Jesus makes it clear that He is referring to *the Father*, and so does John. The nineteenth chapter of Genesis, the twenty-fourth verse, solves then this problem for us once and for all, as even Jehovah's Witnesses will eventually be forced to admit. Moses here reveals a glimpse of the *composite unity* in the triune God. "Then Jehovah rained on Sodom and Gomorrah brimstone and fire *from Jehovah* out of heaven." This unquestionably is the only solution to this dilemma. God the Father rained fire on Sodom and Gomorrah, and God the Son spoke and ate with Abraham and Sarah. Two persons (the third Person of the Trinity is revealed more fully in the New Testament: Jn 14:26; 16:7-14) are both called Jehovah (Gen 18:20; 19:24; cf. Is 9:6; Mic 5:2), and both are *one* (*ECHOD*) with the Holy Spirit in *composite unity* (Deu 6:4). God the Father was in heaven, God the Son died on the cross, God the Holy Spirit comforts the church till Jesus shall come again. This is the triune God, whom Jehovah's Witnesses are committed to ridicule, berate, and blaspheme in the name of "human reason." God said in Genesis 1:26, "Let us make man in *our* image after *our* likeness" (KJV), not in *My* image, after *My* likeness. Here plurality is seen, obviously, God speaking to His coeternal Son (Christ) and addressing *Him* as an *equal*. Genesis 11:7, 9, with reference to the tower of Babel, also lends strong support to the triune God doctrine, where God, speaking as an *equal* to His Son, declares, "Let *us* go down and confound the languages"—plurality and equality. (See also Is 48:16.) In the face of all these texts, the Watchtower is strangely silent. They, however, rally afresh to the attack on page 23 of their article and declare that "there is no basis for concluding that the Holy Spirit is a person." This is so immature and unskilled an attack that it hardly justifies an effort to refute it. The fact that the Holy Spirit is referred to as a person in the masculine gender throughout the New Testament, that He also is described as possessing an active *will* ("If I go not away, the Comforter will not come to you," Jn 16:7, KJV), which is the most concrete trait of a distinct personality, and that He is said to exercise the characteristics of a *teacher* (Jn 16:13), apparently all falls on deaf ears where the

Watchtower is concerned. The literature of Jehovah's Witnesses is also consistently filled with nonsensical questions such as, "How could the one hundred and twenty persons at Pentecost be baptized with a Person?" (Ac 1:5; 2:1-4). In answer to this, it evidently escapes the ever zealous Russellites that the fulfillment of Jesus' prophecy as recorded in Acts 1:5 was explained in chapter two, verse four. Luke here says, "And they were all filled (*Eplesthesan*, Greek) with the Holy Spirit." Jesus obviously did not mean that the apostles would be "immersed" in a person, but filled with and immersed in the power of His presence as symbolized in the tongues like unto fire. If Jehovah's Witnesses ever studied the Scriptures in the open with good scholars and stopped masquerading as biblical authorities, which they are not, it might be interesting to see the results. Of course, great scholarship is not necessary to obtain a saving knowledge of Jesus Christ from God's Word; but when people deny the historic Christian faith and berate those who profess it, they ought to have some scholastic support, and Jehovah's Witnesses have none. The Watchtower widely cries that they will meet all persons with an open Bible, but to this date not one of their alleged authorities has materialized despite our numerous invitations. We of orthodox Christianity do not desire maliciously to attack any one's faith for the "joy" of doing it; but we must be faithful to our Lord's command to "preach the word and contend for the faith."

8

The New World Translations of the Bible

IN ANY DEALINGS one may have with the Watchtower or its numerous representatives, it is a virtual certainty that sooner or later in the course of events the Watchtower's "translations" of the Bible will confront the average prospective convert. These "translations" are titled, *The New World Translation of the Christian Greek Scriptures* and *The New World Translation of the Hebrew Scriptures*.

First published in 1950 and later revised in 1951 and 1961, the New Testament version of these translations sold over 480,000 copies before its initial revision, and at this writing international distribution is calculated in seven figures. The Old Testament version of the first eight books, titled "The Octateuch," had a first edition of 500,000 copies and bids fair to rival its older brother in distribution. These books possess a veneer of scholarship unrivaled for its daring and boldness in a field that all informed scholars know Jehovah's Witnesses are almost totally unprepared to venture into. As a matter of fact, the authors have been able to uncover partially a carefully guarded Watchtower secret: the names of five of the members of the New World Translation committee. Not one of these five people has any training in Greek.*

Be that as it may, however, the "translations" exist and, as has been shown, have had and are having wide distribution both in the continental United States, Canada, and all of the six continents. Jehovah's Witnesses boast that their translations are "the work of competent scholars" and further that they "give a clarity to the Scriptures that other translations have somehow failed to supply." Such stupendous claims by the Watchtower involves

*See Appendix.

the necessity of a careful examination of their translations so that they may be weighed by the standards of sound biblical scholarship. Quite naturally, owing to the length of a normal book chapter, any exhaustive analysis of these works is impossible, but we have selected some of the outstanding errors from the New Testament version.

In their foreword to the *New World Translation of the Christian Greek Scriptures*, the translation committee of the Watchtower claims for itself and its translation a peculiar freedom from what they define as "the misleading influence of religious traditions which have their roots in paganism." This "influence," the Watchtower insists, has colored the inspired Word of God, so it is necessary for them, Jehovah's chosen theocratic representatives, to set aright the numerous alleged examples of "human traditionalism" evidenced in all translations from John Wycliffe to the Revised Standard Version. Should anyone question that this arrogant attitude is the true Watchtower position regarding other translations, the following quote from their foreword will dismiss all doubt:

> But honesty compels us to remark that, while each of them has its points of merit, they have fallen victim to the power of human traditionalism in varying degrees. Consequently, religious traditions, hoary with age, have been taken for granted and gone unchallenged and uninvestigated. These have been interwoven into the translations to color the thought. In support of a preferred religious view, an inconsistency and unreasonableness have been insinuated into the teachings of the inspired writings.
>
> The Son of God taught that the traditions of creed-bound men made the commandments and teachings of God of no power and effect. The endeavor of the New World Bible Translation Committee has been to avoid this snare of religious traditionalism.

From this pompous pronouncement, it is only too evident that the Watchtower considers its scholars the superiors of such great scholars as Wycliffe and Tyndale, not to mention the hundreds of brilliant, consecrated Christian men who produced the King James, American Standard, and New American Standard versions of the Bible. Such a pretext is, of course, too absurd to merit refutation, but let it be remembered that the Watchtower Translation Committee, comparatively speaking, had but a handful of scholars who hold degrees in New Testament Greek exegesis, or Hebrew, for that matter; yet these men dare to challenge the record of translations which have had hundreds of the greatest Greek and Hebrew scholars in the world as contributors.

However, the Watchtower translation speaks for itself and shows more clearly than pen can, the scholastic dishonesty and lack of scholarship within its covers. In order to point out these glaring inconsistencies, the authors have listed five prime examples of the Watchtower's inaccuracies from the New Testament, discussion of which makes up the remainder of this chapter, and upon which we have numerous times asked representatives of the Watchtower to comment, without success.

The first major error we shall discuss is that Jehovah's Witnesses have restored the divine name "Jehovah" to the text of the New Testament. But let us observe this pretext as they stated it in their own words.

"The evidence is, therefore, that the original text of the Christian Greek Scriptures has been tampered with, the same as the text of the LXX* has been. And, at least from the third century A.D. onward, the divine name in tetragrammaton† form has been eliminated from the text by copyists. . . . In place of it they substituted the words *kyrios* (usually translated 'the Lord') and theos, meaning 'God'" (NWT, p. 18).

The "evidence" that the Witnesses refer to is a recently discovered papyrus roll of the LXX which contains the second half of the book of Deuteronomy and which does have the tetragrammaton throughout. Further than this, the Witnesses refer to Aquila (A.D. 128) and Origen who both utilized the tetragrammaton in their respective Version and Hexapla. Jerome in the fourth century also mentioned the tetragrammaton as appearing in certain Greek volumes even in his day. On the basis of this small collection of fragmentary evidence, Jehovah's Witnesses conclude their argument: "It proves that the original LXX did contain the divine name wherever it occurred in the Hebrew original. Considering it a sacrilege to use some substitute such

---

*The Septuagint is a Greek translation of the Old Testament.
†The Hebrew consonants *YHWH*, usually rendered "Jehovah."

as *kyrios* or *theos*, the scribes inserted the tetragammaton at its proper place in the Greek version text" (NWT, p. 12).

The whole case the Witnesses try to prove is that the original LXX and the New Testament autographs all used the tetragrammaton (NWT, p. 18) but owing to "tampering," all these were changed; hence their responsibility to restore the divine name. Such is the argument, and a seemingly plausible one, to those not familiar with the history of manuscripts and the Witnesses' subtle use of terms.

To explain this error of translation is an elementary task. It can be shown from literally thousands of copies of the Greek New Testament that not *once* does the tetragrammaton appear, not even in Matthew, possibly written in Hebrew or Aramaic originally, and therefore more prone than all the rest to have traces of the divine name in it—yet it does not! Beyond this, the roll of papyrus (LXX), which contains the latter part of Deuteronomy and the divine name only proves that one copy did have the divine name (*YHWH*), whereas all other existing copies use *kyrios* and *theos*, which the Witnesses claim are "substitutes." The testimonies of Aquila, Origen, and Jerome, in turn, only show that *sometimes* the divine name was used, but the general truth, upheld by all scholars, is that the Septuagint, with minor exceptions, always uses *kyrios* and *theos* in place of the tetragrammaton, and the New Testament never uses it at all. Relative to the nineteen "sources" the Watchtower uses (NWT, pp. 30-33) for restoring the tetragrammaton to the New Testament, it should be noted that they are all translations from Greek (which uses *kyrios* and *theos*, not the tetragrammaton) back into Hebrew, the earliest of which is A.D. 1385, and therefore they are of no value as evidence.

No scholar, of course, objects to the use of the term *Jehovah* in the Bible. But since only the Hebrew consonants *YHWH* appear without vowels, pronunciation is at best uncertain, and to settle dogmatically on *Jehovah* is straining at the bounds of good linguistics. All students of Hebrew know that any vowel can be inserted between the consonants (*YHWH* or *JHVH*), so that theoretically, the divine name could be any combination from JoHeVaH to JiHiViH without doing violence to the grammar of the language in the slightest degree.

A second problem is found in Colossians 1:16: "By means of him all *other* things were created in the heavens and upon the earth, the things visible and the things invisible, no matter whether they are thrones or Lordships or governments or authorities" (NWT).

In this particular rendering, Jehovah's Witnesses attempt one of the most clever perversions of the New Testament texts that the authors have ever seen. Knowing full well that the word *other* does not occur in this text, or for that matter in any of the three texts (vv. 16, 17, 18), the Witnesses deliberately insert it into the translation in a vain attempt to make Christ a creature and one of the "things" He is spoken of as having created.

Attempting to justify this unheard of travesty upon the Greek language and simple honesty, the New World Translation committee inserts a footnote, marked (a) after each use of the word *other*, which refers the reader to Luke 13:2, 4, "and elsewhere," for apparent support of their ungrammatical rendering. Upon turning to Luke 13:2, 4, however, the elementary Greek student can see that the Witnesses plainly do not have any grammatical leg to stand on as is shown by their immature reasoning. The two verses in Luke utilized by the Watchtower to cover up their scholastic dishonesty are given as follows in the New World Translation.

"So in reply, he said to them: 'Do you imagine that these Galileans were proved worse sinners than all *other* Galileans because they have suffered these things?' (v. 2).

" 'Or those eighteen upon whom the tower of Siloam fell, thereby killing them, do you imagine that they were proved greater debtors than all *other* men inhabiting Jerusalem?' " (v. 4).

In these verses, the Watchtower translators also inserted the word *other*, not present in the Greek text, on the ground that it is implied in the context, owing to the comparison made by Jesus. It is admissible, of course, that Jesus was drawing a contrast between certain Galileans and their fellow countrymen; but it is not admissible to insert terms in order to prove a doctrinal point, and in Colossians 1:15-17, no such comparison or contrast is being made anyway; unless, as is the case with Jehovah's Witnesses, one assumes that Christ Himself was a "creature" or a "thing," which would necessitate inserting the word *other* in order to conform Scripture to a preconceived theology. It is incorrect grammar, no reputable translation dares tamper with doctrinal texts in this way, and not one single competent Greek authority can be cited for this deliberate attempt to reduce the Son of God from Creator to creature.

The entire context of Colossians 1:15-22 is filled with superlatives in its description of the Lord Jesus as the "image of the invisible God, the first-begetter [or, "original bringer forth," Erasmus] of every creature." The apostle Paul lauds the Son of God as Creator of all things (v. 16) and describes Him as existing "before all things" and "holding together all things" (v. 17). This is in perfect harmony with the entire picture Scripture paints of the eternal Word of God (Jn 1:1) who was made flesh (Jn 1:14) and of whom it was written: "All things were made by him, and without him was nothing made that was made" (Jn 1:3). The writer of the book of Hebrews also pointed out that God's Son "upholdeth all things by the word of his power" (Heb 1:3, KJV), and that He is deity in all its fullness, even as Paul wrote to the Colossians: "For ... in him should all the fullness [of God] dwell" (Col 1:19, ASV).

The Scriptures, therefore, bear unmistakable testimony to the creative activity of God's Son, distinguishing Him from among the "things" created, as *the* Creator and Sustainer of "all things."

Jehovah's Witnesses have no conceivable ground, then, for this dishonest rendering of Colossians 1:16, 17, and 18 by the insertion of the word *other*, since they are supported by no grammatical authorities, nor do they dare dispute their perversions with competent scholars lest they further parade their obvious ignorance of Greek exegesis.

A third easily explainable error is found in the *New World Translation's* version of Matthew 27:50: "Again Jesus cried out with a loud voice and ceased to breathe." Or, as it reads in Luke 23:46: "And Jesus called with a loud voice and said: Father, into your hands I entrust my spirit."

For many years, the Watchtower has been fighting a vain battle to redefine biblical terms to suit their own peculiar theological interpretations. They have had some measure of success in this attempt in that they have taught their readers a new meaning for sound biblical terms, and it is this trait of their deceptive system that we analyze now in connection with the above quoted verses.

Matthew 27:50 and Luke 23:46 are parallel passages describing the same event, namely the crucifixion of Jesus Christ. In Matthew's account, the Witnesses had no difficulty substituting the verb *to breathe* for the Greek *pneuma* (spirit), for in their vocabulary, this word has many meanings, none of them having any bearing upon the general usage of the term, biblically, that is, that of an immaterial cognizant nature, inherent in man by definition and descriptive of angels through creation. Jehovah's Witnesses reject this immaterial nature in man and call it "breath," "life," "mental disposition," or "something wind-like." In fact they will call it anything but what God's Word says it is, an invisible nature, eternal by creation, a spirit, made in the image of God (Gen 1:27). We would be poor scholars indeed if we did not point out that sometimes and in various contexts, spirit (*pneuma*) can mean some of the things the Witnesses hold, but context determines translation, along with grammar, and their translations quite often do not remain true to either.

Having forced the word *breathe* into Matthew's account of the crucifixion, to make it appear that Jesus only stopped breathing and did not yield up His invisible nature upon dying, the Witnesses go on to Luke's account, only to be caught in their own trap. Luke, learned scholar and master of Greek that he was, forces the Witnesses to render his account of Christ's words using the correct term *spirit* (*pneuma*), instead of *breathe*, as in Matthew 27:50. Thus in one fell swoop, the entire Watchtower fabric of manufactured terminology collapses, because Jesus would hardly have said: "Father into thy hands I commit my *breath*"; yet if the Witnesses are consistent, which they seldom are, why did they not render the identical Greek term (*pneuma*) as "breath" both times, for it is a parallel account of the same scene!

The solution to this question is quite elementary. The Witnesses could not render it "breath" in Luke and get away with it, so they used it where they could and hoped nobody would notice it, or the different rendering in Matthew. The very fact that Christ dismissed His spirit proves the survival of the human spirit beyond the grave, or as Solomon so wisely put it: "Then shall the dust return to the earth as it was: and the spirit [*pneuma*, LXX] shall return unto God who gave it" (Ec 12:7, KJV).

The fourth problem we shall consider is found in Philippians 1:21-23: "For in my case to live is Christ, and to die, gain. Now if it be to live on in the flesh, this is a fruitage of my work—and yet which thing to choose I do not know. I am under pressure from these two things; but what I do desire is the releasing and the being with Christ, for this, to be sure, is far better" (NWT).

In common with other cults that teach soul-sleep after the death of the body, Jehovah's Witnesses translate texts contradicting this view to suit their own ends, a prime example of which is their rendering of Philippians 1:21-23. The translation, "But what I do desire is the releasing" (v. 23), signifies either a woeful ignorance of the rudiments of the Greek language or a deliberate, calculated perversion of terminology.

It is no coincidence that this text is a great "proof" passage for the expectation of every true Christian who, after death, goes to be with the Lord (2 Co 5:8). Jehovah's Witnesses realize that if this text goes unchanged or unchallenged, it destroys utterly their Russellite teaching that the soul becomes extinct at the death of the body. This being the case, and since they could not challenge the text without exploding the myth of their acceptance of the Bible as the final authority, the Watchtower committee chose to alter the passage in question, give it a new interpretation, and remove this threat to their theology.

The rendering, "But what I do desire is the releasing," particularly the last word, is a gross imposition upon the principles of Greek exegesis because the untutored Russellites have rendered the first aorist active infinitive of the verb *analuoo* (*analusai*) as a substantive (the releasing), which in this context is unscholarly and atrocious Greek. In order to translate it "the releasing" the form would have to be the participle construction (*analusas*), which when used with the word "wish" or "desire" denotes "a great longing" or "purpose" and must be rendered "to depart" or "to unloose." (See the respective lexicons or concordances by Thayer, Liddell & Scott, Strong, Young, and A. T. Robertson.)

It may appear that we have gone to a great deal of trouble just to refute the wrong usage of a Greek form, but in truth, this simple switching of terms is used by the Witnesses in an attempt to teach that Paul meant something entirely different than what he wrote to the Philippians. To see just how the Watchtower manages this, we quote from their own Appendix to the New World Translation (pp. 780-81).

> The verb *a-na-ly'sai* is used as a verbal noun here. It occurs only once more in the Christian Greek Scriptures, and that is at Luke 12:36, where it refers to Christ's return. The related noun (*a-na'-ly-sis*) occurs but once, at II Timothy 4:6, where the apostle says: "The due time for my releasing is imminent." . . . But here at Philippians 1:23 we have not rendered the verb as "returning" or "departing," but as "releasing." The reason is, that the word may convey two thoughts, the apostle's own releasing to be with Christ at His return and also the Lord's releasing Himself from the heavenly restraints and returning as He promised.
>
> In no way is the apostle here saying that immediately at his death he would be changed into spirit and would be with Christ forever. . . . It is to this return of Christ and the apostle's releasing to be always with the Lord that Paul refers at Philippians 1:23. He says there that two things are immediately possible for him, namely, (1) to live on in the flesh and (2) to die. Because of the circumstances to be considered, he expressed himself as being under pressure from these two things, not knowing which thing to choose as proper. Then he suggests a third thing, and this thing he really desires. There is no question about this desire for this thing as preferable, namely, the releasing, for it means his being with Christ.
>
> The expression to *a-na-ly'sai*, or *the releasing* cannot therefore be applied to the apostle's death as a human creature and his departing thus from this life. It must refer to the events at the time of Christ's return and second presence, that is to say, his second coming and the rising of all those dead in Christ to be with him forevermore.

Here after much grammatical intrigue, we have the key as to why the Witnesses went to so much trouble to render *depart* as "releasing." By slipping in this grammatical error, the Watchtower hoped to "prove" that Paul was not really discussing his impending death and subsequent reunion with Christ at all (a fact every major biblical scholar and translator in history has held), but a *third* thing, namely, "the events at the time of Christ's return and second presence." With breathtaking dogmatism, the Witnesses claim that "the releasing cannot therefore be applied to the Apostle's death. It *must* refer to the events at the time of Christ's return." This finds no support in any Greek text or reputable grammatical authority. Contrary to the Watchtower's statement that "The word may convey two thoughts, the Apostle's 'releasing' to be with Christ at his return, and also the Lord's 'releasing' himself from the heavenly restraints and returning as he promised" (NWT, p. 781), the Greek text offers no such thought. As a matter of plain exegetical fact, Christ's return is not even the subject of discussion—rather it is the apostle's death and his concern for the Philippians that is here portrayed. That Paul never expected to "sleep" in his grave until the resurrection, as Jehovah's Witnesses maintain, is evident by the twenty-first verse of the chapter, literally, "For to me to live is Christ, and to die is gain." There would be no gain in dying if men slept till the resurrection for, He is not the God of the dead but the God of the living" (Mk 12:27, KJV). Clearly then, Paul was speaking of but two things: his possible death and subsequent presence with the Lord (2 Co 5:8), and also the possibility of his continuing on in the body, the latter being "more needful" for the Philippian Christians. His choice in his own words was between these two (v. 23), and Jehovah's Witnesses have gone to great trouble for nothing; the Greek text still records faithfully what the inspired apostle said—not what the Watchtower maintains he said.

Concluding our comments upon these verses in Philippians, we feel constrained to point out a final example of Watchtower error relative to Greek translation.

On page 781 of the *New World Translation,* it will be recalled that the committee wrote: "The expression to *a-na-ly'-sai* or *the releasing* cannot therefore apply to the apostle's death as a human creature and his departing thus from this life."

If the reader should turn to page 626 of the same Watchtower translation, he will observe that in 2 Timothy 4:6, the Witnesses once more use the term *releasing* (*analuseos*), where all translators are agreed that it refers to Paul's impending death. The Revised Standard Version, often appealed to by Jehovah's Witnesses, puts it this way:

"For I am already on the point of being sacrificed; the time of my departure has come." (See also, J. N. Darby, *The 'Holy Scriptures' A New Translation from the Original Languages;* Edgar J. Goodspeed, *The New Testament: An American Translation;* King James Version; James Moffatt, *The New Testament, A New Translation;* Joseph B. Rotherham, *The Emphasized New Testament.*)

Jehovah's Witnesses themselves render the text: "For I am already being poured out like a drink offering, and the due time of my *releasing* is imminent" (2 Ti 4:6, NWT).

Now, since it is admitted by the Witnesses under the pressure of every translator's rendering of his text, that it refers to Paul's death and further, since the noun form of the Greek word (*analuseos*) is here used and translated "releasing," why is it that they claim on page 781 that this expression "the releasing" (*analusai,* Phil 1:23) "cannot therefore apply to the apostle's death as a human creature and his departing thus from this life"? The question becomes more embarrassing when it is realized that Jehovah's Witnesses themselves admit that these two forms (*analusai* and *analuseos*) are "related" (p. 781). Hence they have no excuse for maintaining in one place (Phil 1:23) that "the releasing" cannot refer to the apostle's death, and in another place (2 Ti 4:6) using a form of the same word, and allowing that it does refer to his death.

The final misinterpretation that we shall consider from the Watchtower comes from Matthew 24:3. "While he was sitting upon the mount of Olives, the disciples approached him privately, saying: 'Tell us, When will these things be, and what will be the sign of your presence and of the consummation of the system of things?'" (NWT).

Since the days of Pastor Russell and Judge Rutherford, one of the favorite dogmas of the Watchtower has been that of the *parousia*, the second coming or "presence" of the Lord Jesus

Christ. Jehovah's Witnesses have tenaciously clung to the pastor's theology in this respect and maintain that in 1914, when the "times of the gentiles" ended (according to Russell), the "second presence" of Christ began. From the year 1914 onward, the Witnesses maintain,

> Christ has turned his attention toward earth's affairs and is dividing the peoples and educating the true Christians in preparation for their survival during the great storm of Armageddon, when all unfaithful mankind will be destroyed from the face of the earth.[1]

For Jehovah's Witnesses, then, Christ is not coming; He is here! (A.D. 1914)—only invisibly—and He is directing His activities through His theocratic organization in Brooklyn, New York. In view of this claim, it might be well to hearken unto the voice of Matthew who wrote:

> Then if any man shall say unto you, Lo, here is Christ, or there; believe it not. For there shall arise false Christs, and false prophets, and shall shew great signs and wonders; insomuch that, if it were possible, they shall deceive the very elect. Behold, I have told you before. Wherefore if they shall say unto you, Behold he is in the desert; go on forth: behold, he is in the secret chambers; believe it not. For as the lightning cometh out of the east, and shineth even unto the west; so shall also the coming of the Son of man be (Mt 24:23-27, KJV).

Jehovah's Witnesses in their *New World Translation* (p. 780) list the twenty-four occurrences of the Greek word *parousia*, which they translate each time as "presence." They give the following defense for this:

> The tendency of many translators is to render it here "coming" or "arrival." But throughout the twenty-four occurrences, the Greek word PAROUSIA. . . . we have rendered it "presence." From the comparison of the parousia of the Son of man with the days of Noah at Matthew 24:37-39, *it is very evident that the meaning of the word is as we have* rendered it. And from the contrast that is made between the presence and the absence of the apostle both at II Corinthians 10:10-11 and at Philippians 2:12, *the meaning of parousia is so plain that it is beyond dispute by other translators* (NWT, p. 779).

Following this gigantic claim, namely, that their translation of the word *parousia* is "beyond dispute by other translators," the theocratic authorities proceed to list the verses in question.

Now the main issue in debate from a translation standpoint is not the use of the word *presence* for *parousia*, because in some contexts it is certainly allowable (see 1 Co 16:17; 2 Co 7:6-7; 10:10; and Phil 1:26; 2:12). But there are other contexts where it cannot be allowed in the way Jehovah's Witnesses use it, because it not only violates the contextual meaning of the word, but the entire meaning of the passages as always held by the Christian church.

Jehovah's Witnesses claim scholarship for this blanket translation of *parousia*, yet not one great scholar in the history of Greek exegesis and translation has ever held this view. Since 1871, when Pastor Russell produced this concept, upon examination, it has been denounced by every competent scholar.

The reason this Russellite rendering is so dangerous is that it attempts to prove that *parousia*, in regard to Christ's second advent, really means that His return or "presence" was to be invisible and unknown to all but "the faithful" (Russellites, of course).[3]

The New World translators, therefore, on the basis of those texts where it is acceptable to render *parousia* "presence," conclude that it must be acceptable in all texts. But while it appears to be acceptable grammatically, no one but Jehovah's Witnesses or their sympathizers accepts the New World blanket use of "presence," be the translators Christian or not. It simply is not good grammar, and it will not stand up under comparative exegesis, as will be shown. To conclude that *presence* necessarily implies invisibility is also another flaw in the Watchtower's argument, for in numerous places where they render *parousia* "presence," the persons spoken of were hardly invisible. (See 1 Co 16:17, 2 Co 2:12; 7:6; and 10:10.)

If the Watchtower were to admit for one moment that *parousia* can be translated "coming" or "arrival," in the passages which speak of Christ's return the way all scholarly translators render it, then Pastor Russell's "invisible presence" of Christ would

explode in their faces. Hence their determination to deny what
all recognized Greek authorities have established.

Dr. Joseph H. Thayer, who, incidentally, denied the visible
second coming of Christ, says when speaking of *parousia*: "a
return (Phil. 1:26) . . . In the New Testament especially of the
Advent, i.e., the future visible return from heaven of Jesus, the
Messiah, to raise the dead, hold the last judgment, and set up
formally and gloriously the Kingdom of God."[4] (For further
references, see Liddell & Scott, Strong, and any other reputable
authority.)

Dr. Thayer, it might be mentioned again, was honest enough
to say what the New Testament Greek taught, even though he
did not believe it. One could wish that Jehovah's Witnesses were
at least that honest, but they are not!

In concluding this discussion of the misuse of *parousia*, we shall
discuss the verses Jehovah's Witnesses use to "prove" that Christ's
return was to be an invisible "presence" instead of a visible,
glorious, verifiable event.

The following references and their headings were taken from
the book, *Make Sure Of All Things*, published by the Watchtower as an official guide to their doctrine.

> Angels Testified at Jesus' Ascension as a Spirit that Christ
> Would Return in Like Manner, Quiet, Unobserved by the Public
> [p. 320].
>
> Acts 1:9, 11—"And after he had said these things while they
> (only the disciples) were looking on, he was lifted up and a
> cloud caught him up from their vision. . . . 'Men of Galilee, why
> do you stand looking into the sky? This Jesus who was received
> up from you into heaven will come thus in the same manner as
> you have behold him going into heaven.'"

It is quite unnecessary to refute in detail this open perversion
of a clear biblical teaching, because, as John 20:27 clearly shows,
Christ was not a spirit, and did not ascend as one. The very text
they quote shows that the disciples were "looking on" and saw
Him "lifted up and a cloud caught him from their vision" (v. 9).
They could hardly have been looking at a spirit, which by definition is incorporeal (even angels have to take a human form in
order to be seen, Gen 19:1-2), not with human eyes at least, and

Christ had told them once before, "Behold my hands and my feet, that it is I myself: handle me, and see; for a spirit hath not flesh and bones, as ye see me have" (Lk 24:39, KJV).

So it remains for Christ Himself to denounce the Russellite error that He "ascended as a spirit." Moreover, since He left the earth visibly from the Mount of Olives, it is certain that He will return visibly even as the Scriptures teach (see Dan 7:13-14; Mt 24:7-8, 30; 26:63-64; Rev 1:7-8.)

> Christ's Return Invisible, as He Testified that Man Would Not See Him Again in Human Form [p. 321].
>
> John 14:19—"A little longer and the world will behold me no more."
>
> Matthew 23:39—For I say to you, You will by no means see me from henceforth until you say, "Blessed is he that comes in Jehovah's name!" (NWT)

These two passages in their respective contexts give no support to the Russellite doctrine of an invisible "presence" of Christ for two reasons:

First, John 14:19 refers to Christ's anticipated death and resurrection—the "little longer" He made reference to could only have referred to His resurrection and subsequent ascension (Ac 1:9, 11), before which time and during the period following His resurrection, He appeared only to believers, not the world (or unbelievers), hence the clear meaning of His words. Jesus never said that *no* one would ever "see Him again in human form," as the Watchtower likes to make out. Rather in the same chapter, He promised to *"come again* and receive you unto myself, that where I am, there you may be also" (v. 3). The Bible also is quite clear in telling us that one day by His grace alone, "We shall be like him, for we shall *see* him as he is" (1 Jn 3:2, KJV). So the Watchtower once more is forced to silence by the voice of the Holy Spirit.

Second, Matthew 23:39 really proves nothing at all for the Watchtower's faltering arguments, except that Jerusalem will never see Christ again until it blesses Him in repentance as the anointed of God. Actually, the text hurts the Russellite position, for it teaches that Christ will be *visible* at His coming, else they could not see Him to bless Him in the name of the Lord. Christ also qualified the statement with the word *until,* a definite reference to His visible second advent (Mt 24:30).

Early Christians Expected Christ's Return to Be Invisible. Paul Argued There Was Insufficient Evidence in Their Day [p. 321].

II Thessalonians 2:1-3, "However, brothers, respecting the presence of our Lord Jesus Christ and our being gathered together to him, we request of you not to be quickly shaken from your reason nor to be excited either through an inspired expression or through a verbal message or through a letter as though from us, to the effect that the day of Jehovah is here. Let no one seduce you in any manner, because it will not come unless the falling away comes first and the man of lawlessness gets revealed, the son of destruction." (N.W.T.)

This final example from 2 Thessalonians most vividly portrays the Watchtower at its crafty best, as they desperately attempt to make Paul teach what in all his writings he most emphatically denied, namely, that Christ would come invisibly for His saints.

In his epistle to Titus, Paul stressed the importance of "looking for that blessed hope, and the glorious appearing of the great God and our Saviour Jesus Christ" (2:13, KJV), something he would not have been looking for if it was to be a secret, invisible *parousia* or "presence."

Paul, contrary to Jehovah's Witnesses, never believed in an invisible return, nor did any bona fide member of the Christian church, up until the fantasies of Charles Taze Russell and his *parousia* mistake, as a careful look at Paul's first epistle to the Thessalonians plainly reveals. Said the inspired apostle, "For this we say unto you by the word of the Lord, that we which are alive and remain unto the *coming* of the Lord shall not prevent them which are asleep. For the Lord himself shall *descend* from heaven [visible] with a shout [audible], with the voice of the archangel, and with the trump of God: and the dead in Christ shall rise first" (4:15-16, KJV).

Here we see that in perfect accord with Matthew 26 and Revelation 1, Christ is pictured as *coming* visibly, and in this context, no reputable Greek scholar alive will allow the use of "presence"; it must be "coming." (See also 2 Th 2:8.)

For further information relative to this subject, consult any standard concordance and Greek lexicon available, and trace Paul's use of the word *coming.* Paul never entertained the Watchtower's fantastic view of Christ's return.

These things being clearly understood, the interested reader should give careful attention to those verses in the New Testament which do not use the word *parousia* but are instead forms of the verb *elthon* and related to the word *erchomai* (see Thayer) and which refer to the Lord's coming as a visible manifestation. These various texts cannot be twisted to fit the Russellite pattern of "presence," since *erchomai* means "to come," "to appear," "to arrive," in the most definite sense of the term. (For reference, check Mt 24:30 in conjunction with Mt 26:64—*erchomenon;* also Jn 14:3—*erchomai;* and Rev 1:7—*erchetai.*)

Once it is perceived that Jehovah's Witnesses are only interested in what they can make the Scriptures say, and not in what the Holy Spirit has already perfectly revealed, then the careful student will reject entirely Jehovah's Witnesses and their Watchtower translations. These are as "blind leaders of the blind" (Mt 15:14, KJV) who have turned "the grace of God into lasciviousness," and denied the Lord Jesus Christ (Jude 4, KJV). Further, that they "wrest . . . the scriptures unto their own destruction" (2 Pe 3:16, KJV), the foregoing evidence has thoroughly revealed for all to judge.

9

Jehovah's Witnesses and the New Birth

THERE ARE MANY PECULIARITIES to be found within the Jehovah's Witnesses movement which provoke the earnest student of Scripture to profound thoughts at times; for once in a great while, the Watchtower sounds a note of apparent evangelical flavor. Unfortunately, these scattered "notes" are revealed to be pseudo-evangelical when one thoroughly understands the Witnesses' mangled jargon. Sad to say, this jargon often dupes many into labeling the zealous disciples of Pastor Russell as "fundamentalists," a term not even vaguely applicable to Jehovah's Witnesses.

One of these "evangelical" notes was sounded in an article entitled, "Are You Born Again?" an article which portrays the Witnesses at their crafty best in the polished art of "term-switching," of which they are past masters. In this article, under the heading, "How Born Again," the Witnesses give this summary of what it means to be "born again" and the scriptural position regarding the new birth. To illustrate this Watchtower chicanery, we quote from this subhead, which is one of their best pieces of pseudoevangelical material:

> Since all these are sinners, for them to be born again they must "repent and turn around," something Jesus did not have to do, as he was not a sinner. But that is not enough, for by their own efforts they have no standing before God as Jesus did as a perfect man. They can, however, have such a righteous standing imputed to them by exercising faith in Jesus' blood that was shed for them. On the basis of their exercising faith in Christ's blood and dedicating themselves to do God's will, God declares them righteous and brings them forth or acknowledges them as his

spiritual sons with the hope of life in the heavens with Christ.—
Acts 3:19; Romans 5:1.

Since this being born again is dependent upon their knowledge of God's will and purpose toward them as revealed in his
Word, and upon the action of God's spirit upon them, it is said
that these are "born from water and spirit," the water being a
symbol of God's Word. (John 3:5, 6, *New World Trans.;* Ephesians 5:26). That the literal water of baptism is not the thing
that marks one's being born again is apparent from Cornelius'
experience. He received God's holy spirit, thereby being born
again as a spiritual son of God, before he was baptized.—Acts,
chapter 10.

Being born again brings with it many responsibilities. It
requires of one that he "bear witness to the truth," even as Jesus
did. It also requires bringing forth "the fruitage of the spirit,"
which "is love, joy, peace, longsuffering, kindness, goodness,
faith, mildness, self-control." It also means the avoidance of the
practice of sin.—John 18:37; Galatians 5:22, 23; I John 3:9, *New
World Trans.*[1]

From this apparently evangelical presentation, the careless
reader might deduce that the Watchtower, like the proverbial
leopard, had finally changed its spots, but such is not the case
at all.

In the paragraphs following this attempt at orthodoxy, the
Witnesses overstep themselves and reveal clearly what "born
again" really means to them and, more important, to whom it
exclusively applies.

The Scriptures also speak of those having been born again as
"begotten of God," as having "received a spirit of adoption as
sons" and as "a new creation." Compared with all those eventually gaining salvation these are but, as Jesus calls them, a "little
flock," just the 144,000 that the apostle John saw standing on
Mount Zion with Christ Jesus, the 144,000 that were sealed from
the twelve tribes of spiritual Israel.—Romans 8:15; Revelation
7:4; 14:1, 3, *New World Trans.*

Salvation for Others Also

Only 144,000 born again and to receive the heavenly reward?
Yes. Does that mean that only so few will ever gain salvation?
Not at all, for John saw not only 144,000 sealed but also "a great
crowd, which no man was able to number, out of all nations and

tribes and people and tongues." These also experience salvation, for they are heard saying: "Salvation we owe to our God, who is seated on the throne, and to the Lamb." Those born again with Christ Jesus will serve as kings, as priests, as judges and as the seed of Abraham that will bless all the families of the earth, namely, the rest of mankind who will gain salvation, including the great crowd that John saw.[2]

Here then is the true Watchtower position on this great biblical doctrine. Note that only the "little flock," the 144,000 faithful Jehovah's Witnesses, or "spiritual Israel," are the ones designated as "born again." These are members of a special heavenly class who will see the kingdom of God and live forever as "spirit beings." The balance of "faithful" persons, who by then will have been received into the Russellite fold, will dwell forever in happiness upon the earth, and these are designated as "the great crowd"—mentioned in Revelation 7:9. Those great patriarchs of the Old Testament, as well as all faithful followers of Jehovah before Christ, can never be "born again" or entitled to entrance into the kingdom of heaven, the Witnesses tell us, since they are sleeping in their graves until the resurrection, when they will rise to become what they term "princes in all the earth." Jehovah's Witnesses further believe that "the number still on earth who have been born again is decreasing while the number of those having earthly hopes is increasing. According to the 1955 *Yearbook of Jehovah's Witnesses,* there are about 580,498 dedicated Christian ministers of Jehovah but only 17,884 who profess to be of the number born again.[3]

From this composite picture of Watchtower theological double-talk, it is fairly easy to assume that more error must enter their theory before they bring it to fruition, and so it does in their concept of Christ and the relationship He maintained relative to the "second birth."

According to Jehovah's Witnesses, Jesus was Himself "born again"—at the Jordan, at which time He said: "'Look! I am coming to do your [God's] will,'" giving public testimony thereto by being baptized. There God brought Him forth as a spiritual Son by bestowing His Holy Spirit upon Him, it descending in the form of a dove and by "audibly acknowledging Him as His Son, even as we read: 'This is my Son, the beloved, whom I have approved.'—Hebrews 10:9; Matthew 3:17"[4]

The Witnesses complete this grotesque picture when they portray Christ as merely a perfect man who had every possibility of being unfaithful to God that Adam did. Note their very words:

> At this time Jesus was given a *conditional* right to life as a spirit creature in the heavens, dependent upon his *proving faithful* under test. So for three and a half years "he learned obedience from the things he suffered." And after his having proved himself faithful "as far as death, yes, death on a torture stake," "God exalted him to a superior position and kindly gave him the name that is above every other name," so that now he "is the reflection of (God's) glory. So Christ Jesus was the first to be born again. He was born again by God's spirit operating upon him to give him a conditional right to life in the heavens, heavenly life being the purpose of his being born again, or its goal.— Hebrews 5:8; Philippians 2:8, 9; Hebrews 1:3, *New World Trans.*[5]

It is clearly evident from this bold slander of our Lord's deity and purity that Jehovah's Witnesses have no concept of the true meaning of the new birth; otherwise they would know that Jesus never needed a spiritual birth, being the substance of God incarnate (Is 9:6; Mic 5:2; Zec 12:10; Jn 1:1, 14; 8:58; Col 2:9; Titus 2:13; Heb 1:3), literally "a form of God" (Phil 2:6), and hence the Author of eternal life—equal with God, His Father (Jn 5:18).

Contrary to Jehovah's Witnesses' teaching, the Scriptures never recognize their "two-class" method of salvation, nor does the Bible teach that Christ "was given a conditional right to life as a spirit creature in the heavens dependent upon his proving faithful under test."[6] The Bible, in fact, most specifically hails the Messiah as "the true God, and eternal life" (1 Jn 5:20) and commands all men to "honour the Son, even as they honour the Father" (Jn 5:23, KJV). Never for one instant was Christ ever in danger of soiling His humanity by sin as Adam did, for in Jesus Christ, Satan was confronted with the God-man who was "manifested . . . [to] destroy the works of the devil" (1 Jn 3:8, KJV). The great mystery of Christ's two natures and their relationship to temptation will never be solved on this earth, but it is true nonetheless that He "was in all points tempted like as we are, yet without sin" (Heb 4:15, KJV), while at the same time He never ceased being what He ever is—the eternal Word, God the Son, the great "I Am" (Jn 8:58).

Relative to the magic number 144,000 which the Witnesses trumpet so loudly, a coldly logical appraisal of the texts they utilize and the respective contexts, is in order.

Jehovah's Witnesses quote Revelation 7:4 and 14:1, 3 to "prove" that the 144,000 persons therein referred to are none other than the "spiritual class" of loyal Russellites (Pastor Russell and Judge Rutherford are included in this exalted group), who, when they die, are immediately transferred to the heavenly kingdom to be with Christ. The overzealous apostles of confusion should, however, note that the 144,000 persons are *Jews*, not Gentiles, and they are not "spiritual Israel" either, for they are named by tribes, a distinctly Judaistic flavor of earthly origin and application. These 144,000 Jews will come out of the great tribulation, Scripture tells us, and they will have been martyred for their repentant faith in Jesus Christ as Messiah during the reign of Antichrist. (See Jer 30:7; Dan 9:24-27; Mt 24:15; 2 Th 2:4; Rev 3:10; 9:2-11; 11:2-3; 12:12; 13:1; 16.)

Of course, the Watchtower never got this revelation until Pastor Russell "discovered" it, and one can hardly blame them for remaining faithful to his teachings, even though they deny they are following them today.

Let it be remembered, then, that the 144,000 are not a special "heavenly class," and that all men who have trusted Christ, whether through prophetic faith or apostolic testimony, will one day "inherit the kingdom prepared for you from the foundation of the world" (Mt 25:34, KJV). This then is the glorious kingdom of "the great God and our Saviour Jesus Christ" (Titus 2:13, KJV), and not the Russellite pseudoparadise that finds no place in the inspired Word of God and which the ever zealous Jehovah's Witnesses peddle from innumerable street corners the world over as part of their kingdom message.

The Lord Jesus Christ spoke incessantly of the kingdom of heaven and the kingdom of God, but He never once restricted it to 144,000, as do Jehovah's Witnesses. Rather, He taught all men to seek it first, and promised that whoever sought would find.

Jehovah's Witnesses have deliberately perverted the clear teachings of the Scriptures on this point, and we must be most vigilant that their errors do not go unchallenged or unanswered.

Now that we have discussed their interpretation of being born again, let us insert the Christian teaching on this doctrine. Salvation is the result of being "born again" by God's Holy Spirit (Jn 3:3), at which time the repentant sinner becomes in Christ "a new creation . . . the old things pass away, behold all things become new" (2 Co 5:17). We realize then that we are reborn spiritually upon acceptance of Christ as Lord and Saviour, a birth "from above" so to speak, a regeneration of our souls through God's sovereign grace alone, by faith in the "Son of his love" (Col 1:13, KJV). We are redeemed, Scripture tells us, not with "corruptible things, as silver and gold . . . but with the precious blood of Christ" (1 Pe 1:18-19, KJV) who gave Himself "a ransom for all" (1 Ti 2:5-6, KJV) and a sacrifice for "the sins of the whole world" (1 Jn 2:2, KJV). That this marvelous rebirth is essential to eternal salvation, the Scriptures leave no doubt whatsoever (Jn 3:5-6), and that man's redemption is solely a free gift from God (Eph 2:8-9) apart from any human merit, no student of the Bible doubts for a moment.

Quite naturally, there are some groups in Christendom who maintain that "the new birth" is the result of infant baptism, at which time "original sin" is washed away, but from a purely consistent standpoint, this view cannot stand the test of hermeneutics* and hence is rejected as untenable.

It is quite true that the Lord Jesus Christ said, "Except a man be born of water and Spirit he cannot see the kingdom of God" (Jn 3:5, 6), but that He was referring to a baptism of repentance and the coming power of the Holy Spirit in His regenerating ministry is quite clear. There was *no* other baptism but that of repentance, *not* regeneration, a far different matter by any logical standards. Today baptism unto repentance is no more, but a man must still figuratively "be born of water" (repentance) at which

---

*Hermeneutics is the science of comparing all related biblical texts, contexts, and grammar, to arrive at a common teaching.

moment he undergoes a "washing of water" by the Word (Eph 5:26), or a complete regeneration of the soul through the Holy Spirit (Titus 3:5). This in turn fulfills perfectly Christ's description of a birth by "water" (repentance) and "the Spirit," resulting in complete redemption and the guarantee of eternal life in the kingdom of God (Jn 3:3, 16, 36; 5:24; 6:47).

There are others, of course, who equate water with the Holy Spirit ("except a man be born of water, even the spirit") to facilitate an understanding of the text. But one thing is most certain regardless of the modes of explanation, and that is the demonstrable truth that the new birth affects only those who are capable of forming a decision for Christ, who are sufficiently matured to "repent" of sin and "believe unto righteousness." The striving of those who believe in baptismal regeneration to make this text prove infant baptism and the "washing away of original sin" cannot erase the plain declarations of Scripture. Water itself never had the power to cleanse from sin,† "for it is the blood that maketh an atonement for the soul" (Lev 17:11, KJV) and "without shedding of blood is no remission" (Heb 9:22, KJV).

The Lord Jesus Christ guaranteed our new birth and presence in the kingdom of God when He offered one sacrifice for sin forever (Heb 10:12), the sacrifice of Himself through the eternal Spirit for "the whole world" (1 Jn 2:2).

Jehovah's Witnesses, therefore, by denying baptismal regeneration, claim evangelical doctrine, but as can be easily shown, the new birth for them only embraces 144,000 elect members (see Rev 7:4, 14:1) or "spiritual Israel," and the Witnesses today only claim 17,844 persons have entered this class, at least in our era of history. For Jehovah's Witnesses, then, one does not need to be "born again," but merely obedient to the theocratic rule, in order to inherit everlasting life—a teaching completely foreign to the Bible and one that finds no sustained support, even when the text-lifting Russellites attempt to pervert isolated verses.

---

†Some quote Ac 22:16, "Be baptized, and wash away thy sins," as proof that water cleanses sin, however, this text and Acts 2:38 cannot possibly be a literal use of water for the cleansing of sin. Since Paul would have baptized all his converts zealously, but he himself said, "But I thank God that I baptized none of you, but Crispus and Gaius" (1 Co 1:14, KJV).

In view of this one more clever attempt by Jehovah's Witnesses to masquerade as Evangelicals, all true believers in Christ ought always to beware of the Watchtower's subtlety. They have never been "born again," singly or collectively, and they are dangerous to the faith of the innocent and poorly informed.

10

How to Witness to Jehovah's Witnesses

IN DRAWING THIS STUDY of Jehovah's Witnesses to a close, it is expedient and vitally necessary that a clear picture be presented of what this cult means to all Christians. This organization has mushroomed from a meager beginning in 1881 until now it extends to every part of the globe and continues to grow in strength and popularity each year. Because the cult does away with the doctrine of eternal retribution for sin* it appeals greatly to those who believe they see in it an escape from the penalty of personal transgression. Jehovah's Witnesses offer an illusionary "Kingdom" to the personalities who desire importance, and most of all an outlet to vent their wrath upon religious leaders and organizations whose doctrines they assail as "of the Devil."† We do not believe for one moment that the greater body of these people know the true implications of Russell's doctrines, however, let no Jehovah's Witnesses ever disclaim Russellistic origin. Charles Taze Russell founded, operated, propagated, and gave his life to further this cult, and his teachings permeate every major phase of its doctrines, despite the intense aloofness they manifest when his past is mentioned. But now the question arises. How can so many people be deceived by so obviously fraudulent a type of religion? To understand this, the teachings and methods of propagation of the cult must be analyzed.

*"Eternal torture is nowhere taught in the Bible" (C. T. Russell, *The Plan of the Ages*, p. 128).

†J. F. Rutherford, *Deliverance*, pp. 91, 222, 226, 230. "Clergymen forming a part of the World are therefore Enemies of God" (Ibid., p. 91). "The ecclesiastical systems Catholic and Protestant are under the supervision of the Devil . . . and therefore, constitute the Antichrist" (Ibid., pp. 222, 226, 230).

According to them, all religious leaders and organizations are false, and anything they say is to be discounted as the "vain philosophies of men." The Scriptures are always made to conform to Jehovah's Witnesses' beliefs, never Jehovah's Witnesses' beliefs to the Scriptures. Rutherford's legal mind made most of the conjecture and linguistic chicanery reasonable to the minds of the people to whom he addressed it, and his books are masterpieces of illogical and invalid premises and conclusions.

To trace the logic and reasoning processes of Rutherford is the task of a logician, since, for Russell or Rutherford, a contradiction can be a premise which, regardless of the steps, always has a valid conclusion in their system of thinking. Jehovah's Witnesses' doctrine is a mass of half-truths and pseudoscholastic material which, to the untutored mind, appears as wonderful revelation.

Recently, when I was speaking to an ardent Jehovah's Witness, the following statement fell unashamedly from his lips: "I have never met anyone who knows more about Greek than the Society." In all probability he was right, for had he met someone who did know Greek he would never have become a member of the cult. The Society, to our knowledge, does not have any Greek scholars of any repute in their ranks, and if they do, we would welcome any opportunity for them to come out from behind their lexicons and explain their rendition of John 1:1, 8:58 and Colossians 2:9, to mention just a few. Hebrew scholars are also included in this invitation.

Another trait of the Society is their aversion to signing literary efforts such as *"Let God Be True," The Truth Shall Make You Free,* and *The New World Translation.* By not committing names of persons to their particular books, the Society escapes the unpleasant task of having to answer for their numerous blunders. Their standard answer is, "Many persons worked on the books, not just one particular person." In their predicament, having no recognized scholarship behind them, they have chosen the wisest possible course—silence. The plain truth of the matter is that the "new" books are just rephrases of Russell's and Rutherford's works and contain no originality other than up-to-date information on world conditions and new approaches to old material.

One of the distinguishing characteristics of an ardent Jehovah's Witness is his (or her) ability to handle the Scriptures. The *Emphatic Diaglott,* with its interlinear readings of the Greek, facilitates their progress in this project. Any good Jehovah's Witness, sad to say, can cause the average Christian untold trouble in the Scriptures, though the trouble in most cases has an elementary solution. The Christian is bewildered by the glib manner in which they repeat Scripture verses (usually entirely out of context) and sprinkle their discourses with Greek or Hebrew grammatical terms, of which they have no knowledge beyond their *Diaglott.* The boldness with which they collar the unwary pedestrian, intrude on the quiet of a restful evening, attend their conventions, and propagate their literature, is a danger signal that evangelical Christianity would do well to heed and take definite steps to combat. As has been observed, the answer to Jehovah's Witnesses, or "Russellism" if you will, is the deity of Jesus Christ, and in teaching that one cardinal doctrine of the Christian faith, all energy ought to be expended to the uttermost. All ministers, Sunday school supervisors, Bible and Tract Societies and teachers should drill their charges in biblical memorization and doctrinal truths, that a united Christian front may be thrown up against this ever growing menace to sound reasoning in biblical exposition and study. The plan is not difficult, and only procrastination hinders its adoption. This problem is also the task of Christian colleges, seminaries, and Bible schools, who too long have neglected the institution of strong cult courses in their curricula. The fruit of their neglect is before us today. Must we stand by in silence while the Word of God is defamed, the Lordship of Christ blasphemed, and the faith of generations still unborn is threatened by a group of people who will not listen to honest biblical truths, and dare not contest them in scholastic discussion? It is frustrating and exasperating to carry on a discussion with a person or persons who argue in circles and dodge artfully from one refutation to another. These tactics characterize the preaching and argumentation of Jehovah's Witnesses which must be met by calm dispositions and truthful scriptural exegesis on the part of well-grounded Christians. Information in the form of documentary evidence and cold facts has met and can meet their perversions and emerge triumphant over them.

We as Christians must perform this task without delay; we can ill afford to wait any longer.

Selected Terms and Texts Misapplied by Jehovah's Witnesses

To review all the terms and texts which Jehovah's Witnesses have misinterpreted and misapplied to bolster up their fractured system of theology would be impossible in the space available here. Therefore, we have chosen to survey six of their worst perversions of common biblical terms, and various texts which the Watchtower has mauled and mangled almost beyond recognition with little or no regard for hermeneutical principles, contexts, or the laws of sound exegesis. An understanding of these terms as they are used by Jehovah's Witnesses will prove helpful to any Christian confronted by them.

These examples of Watchtower deceptions are found all neatly cataloged in their handbook of doctrinal subjects entitled, *Make Sure of All Things,* upon which this study is principally based, should any care to check further their authenticity.

MISAPPLIED TERMS

Only begotten (*monogenes,* Greek). Jehovah's Witnesses, in their zeal to establish the Christology of Arius of Alexandria, have seized upon this Greek term, translated "only begotten" in the New Testament, and unfortunately, they have been most successful in hoodwinking many uninformed persons into believing that "only begotten" really means "only generated." From this erroneous view, they therefore suggest that since the term is applied to Jesus Christ five times in the New Testament, Christ is but a creature, or as they love to quote Codex Alexandrinus, "The only begotten God" (Jn 1:18).

It should be noted in this connection, therefore, that the most authoritative lexicons and grammar books, not to mention numerous scholarly works, all render *monogenes* as "only or unique 'the only member of a kin or kind, hence generally only.'"[1] Moulton and Milligan in their *Vocabulary of the Greek Testament,* render *monogenes* as "one of a kind, only, unique,"[2] facts that establish beyond scholarly doubt the truth of the contention that in both classical and Koine Greek, the term *monogenes* carries the meaning of "only," "unique," or, "the only members of a particular kind." The Septuagint translation of the Old Testament also utilizes the term *monogenes* as the equivalent in translation of the Hebrew adjective *YACHID* translated "solitary" (Ps 68:6). This interesting fact reveals that the translators understood *monogenes* to have the meaning of uniqueness attached to it, emphasis obviously being placed on "only" and decidedly not on "genus" or "kind."

In other places in the New Testament, such as Luke 7:11-18; 8:42; 9:38; and Hebrews 11:17, the rendering "only begotten" in the sense that Jehovah's Witnesses attempt to employ it in their translations and propaganda is an exegetical impossibility; especially in the instance of Hebrews 11:17, where Isaac is called the "only begotten" son of Abraham. Certainly he was not the eldest child, but rather he was the *sole* or *only* precious son, in the sense that Abraham loved him in a unique way.

Dr. Thayer referring to *monogenes* states, "single of its kind, only . . . used of Christ, denotes the only Son of God."[3] Unfortunately, in ancient literature, *monogenes* became connected with the Latin term *unigenitus*. However, such a translation is basically incorrect, as any lexicographical study will quickly reveal.

The early church Fathers were in essential agreement that Jesus Christ preexisted from all eternity in a unique relationship to God the Father. In the year 325 at the Council of Nicaea, it was officially proclaimed that Jesus Christ was of the same substance or nature as the Father, and those who differed with this pronouncement, which the church had always held, were excommunicated. Among them was Arius of Alexandria, a learned Presbyter and the Christological father of Jehovah's Witnesses. Arius held that Jesus Christ was a created being, the first and greatest creation of God the Father, that He did not preexist from all eternity and that His only claim to Godhood was the fact that He had been created first and then elevated to the rank of a deity.

Arius derived many of his ideas from his teacher, Lucien of Antioch, who in turn borrowed them from Origen who himself had introduced the term *eternal generation* or the concept that

God from all eternity generates a second person like Himself, the "eternal Son." Arius, of course, rejected this as illogical and unreasonable, which it is, and taking the other horn of the dilemma, reduced the eternal Word of God to the rank of a creation! It is a significant fact, however, that in the earliest writings of the church Fathers dating from the first century to the year 230, the term *eternal generation* was never used, but it has been this dogma later adopted by Roman Catholic theology which has fed the Arian heresy through the centuries and today continues to feed the Christology of Jehovah's Witnesses.

In the year A.D. 328, in his private creed, Arius interestingly enough applies the term *gegennemenon* in reference to Christ, not the terms *monogenes* or *ginomai*. *Gegennemenon* is a derivative of the word *gennao* which is translated "begotten" and rightly so; further than this, Eusebius of Caesarea, a follower of Arius, in about 325, also utilized the term *gegennemenon* not *monogenes*, a fact which throws a grammatical monkey wrench into the semantic machinations of the Watchtower.

We may see, therefore, that a study of this term *monogenes* reveals that in itself, it is understood in both the classical and Koine vocabulary to be a term emphasizing uniqueness (the only one, the beloved); and there is no good grammatical ground for insisting, as Jehovah's Witnesses do, that it *must* mean "only generated," that is, "only created."

Regarding the five times in the New Testament where the term *monogenes* is applied to Jesus Christ (Jn 1:14, 18; 3:16, 18; 1 Jn 4:9), it can easily be seen that the proper rendering "only" or "unique," in keeping with the historic usage of the term, in no way disturbs the context, but in fact, makes it clearer Christologically, eliminating the concept fostered by the Arians and carried on by Jehovah's Witnesses that "only begotten" must imply creation, which it most certainly does not!

As we mentioned before, the doctrine of eternal generation relative to the preexistence of the Lord Jesus Christ is one of the great stumbling blocks in any intelligent approach to the Christological problems of the New Testament. This being true, the authors feel it is wiser to return to the original language of Scripture in its description of the Lord Jesus and His preincarnate

existence, where He is never referred to in the Bible, except pro-
phetically, as the "eternal Son" but as the Word of God (Jn 1:1)
who "was" from all eternity and who "became" flesh (Jn 1:14),
taking upon Himself the nature of man, and as such was "begotten" of the virgin Mary by the power of the Holy Spirit. The
"unique," "only" Son of God, then, whose uniqueness stems from
the fact that of all men, He was the most precious in the Father's
sight, beloved above all His brethren, so much so that the Father
could say of Him when He sent Him into the world, "Thou art
my Son, this day have I begotten thee" (Heb 1:5), is not a creature or a demi-god but God over all.

The Bible clearly teaches, then, that Jesus Christ, before His
incarnation, was the eternal Word, wisdom, or Logos, of God,
preexistent from all eternity, coequal, coexistent, coeternal with
the Father, whose intrinsic nature of deity He shared, and even
though clothed in human form, he never ceased to be deity, "God
manifest in the flesh" (1 Ti 3:16) or, as Paul put it so directly, "in
him dwelleth all the fulness of the Godhead bodily" (Col 2:9,
KJV).

By insisting upon the correct title of the preexistent Christ, orthodox Christianity can successfully undercut the emphasis Jehovah's Witnesses place upon *monogenes*, showing in contrast,
that "only begotten" is a term of time which can have no meaning outside of the sphere that man knows as recorded experience;
and further, that Jesus Christ is not called by Scripture the "eternal Son," the error passed on from Origen under the title "eternal
generation." But rather, He is the living Word of God (Heb 4:
12); Creator of the universe (2 Pe 3:5); Sustainer of all things
(2 Pe 3:7); first begotten from the dead (Ac 13:33); and our
"great high priest, that has passed into the heavens, Jesus the
Son of God . . . [who can] be touched with the feelings of our
infirmities, [and who] was in all points tempted like as we are,
yet without sin" (KJV). Let us fix these things in our minds,
then:

1. The doctrine of "eternal generation" or the eternal Sonship
of Christ, which springs from the Roman Catholic doctrine first
conceived by Origen in A.D. 230, is a theory which opened the
door theologically to the Arian and Sabellian heresies which to-

day still plague the Christian church in the realms of Christology.

2. The Scripture nowhere calls Jesus Christ the eternal Son of God, and He is never called Son at all prior to the incarnation, except in prophetic passages in the Old Testament.

3. The term *Son* itself is a functional term, as is the term *Father*, and has no meaning apart from time. The term *Father*, incidentally, never carries the descriptive adjective *eternal* in Scripture; as a matter of fact, only the Spirit is called eternal* ("the eternal Spirit," Heb 9:14), emphasizing the fact that the words *Father* and *Son* are purely functional, as previously stated.

4. Many heresies have seized upon the confusion created by the illogical "eternal Sonship" or "eternal generation" theory of Roman Catholic theology, unfortunately carried over to some aspects of Protestant theology.

5. Finally, there cannot be any such thing as eternal Sonship, for there is a logical contradiction of terminology due to the fact that the word *Son* predicates time and the involvement of creativity. Christ, the Scripture tells us, as the Logos, is timeless, "The *Word* was in the beginning" *not* the Son!

To sum up, the Lord Jesus Christ, true God and true man, is now and for all eternity, Son of God and Son of man; therefore, in this sense, He is the eternal Son; but to be biblical in the true sense of the term, we must be willing to admit that He was known prior to His incarnation as the eternal Word, and knowledge of this fact cuts across the very basic groundwork and foundation of the Arian system of theology espoused by Jehovah's Witnesses. For if *only begotten* means "unique" or "only one of its kind," there cannot be any ground for rendering it "only generated," as Jehovah's Witnesses often attempt to do, in a vain attempt to rob Christ of His deity.

If we relegate the terms *Father* and *Son* to the sphere of time as functional vehicles for the conveyance of the mysterious relationship which existed from all eternity between God and His Word, we will be probing deeper into the truth of the Scripture, which seems to teach us that God calls Christ His eternal Word, lest we should ever forget that He is intrinsic Deity (for never

*The Trinity, as such, is, however, spoken of as "the everlasting God" (Ro 16:26).

was there a moment when God had a thought apart from His Logos or reason). Furthermore, God calls Christ His "Son," lest we should think of the Word as being an impersonal force or attribute instead of a substantive entity existing in a subject-object relationship, the eternal God "who is the Saviour of all men, especially those who believe."

Since the word *Son* definitely suggests inferiority and derivation, it is absolutely essential then that Christ, as the eternal Word, be pointed up as an antidote to the Arian heresy of Jehovah's Witnesses; and in this light, we can understand quite plainly the usages of the term *monogenes* not in the Jehovah's Witnesses' sense of creatureliness but in the true biblical sense of "uniqueness," that is, "the unique or only Son of God," generated in the womb of a woman by the direct agency of the Holy Spirit, "God manifest in the flesh." "The great God and our Saviour Jesus Christ" (Titus 2:13, KJV).

Greater (*meizon,* Greek). Another principal term utilized by Jehovah's Witnesses is the term *greater* translated from the Greek, meizon as it appears in John 14:28, "Ye have heard how I said unto you, I go away, and come again unto you. If ye loved me, ye would rejoice, because I said I go unto the Father: for my Father is greater than I" (KJV). From this particular text, lifted conveniently out of its context by the ever zealous Russellites, the Watchtower attempts to "prove" that since Jesus stated in His own words, while He was on earth, that His Father was "greater" than He was, therefore Christ could not be equal with God or one of the members of the Trinity which Jehovah's Witnesses deny so vehemently.

On the face of the matter, this appears to be a good argument from Christ's usage of the word *greater,* but a closer examination of the context and of the hermeneutical principles which govern any sound exegetical study of the New Testament, quickly reveals that theirs is a shallow case indeed and one which rests rather unsteadily upon one Greek word in a most restricted context.

The refutation of this bit of Watchtower semantic double-talk is found in a comparison with Hebrews 1:4, as "Being made so much *better* than the angels, he hath by inheritance obtained a more excellent name than they" (KJV).

In the first chapter of Hebrews, the verse previously cited, an entirely different word is utilized when comparing Christ and the angels. This word is *kreitton* and is translated "better" in the King James Version. Paralleling these two comparisons, then, that of Jesus with His Father in John 14:28, and Jesus with the angels in Hebrews 1:4, one startling fact immediately attracts attention. In the fourteenth chapter of John, as the Son of man who had emptied Himself of His prerogatives of deity (Phil 2: 8-11), and taken upon Himself the form of a slave, the Lord Jesus Christ could truthfully say, "My Father is greater than I," greater being a *quantitative* term descriptive of *position* and certainly in no sense of the context could it be construed as a comparison of nature or quality.

In the first chapter of Hebrews, however, the comparison made there between the Lord Jesus Christ and angels is clearly one of nature. The Greek *kreitton* being a term descriptive of quality; Christ was *qualitatively* better than the angels because He was their Creator (Col 1:16-17), and as such, He existed before all things, and through Him all things hold together (Col 1:17-19). Since His intrinsic nature is that of deity (Jn 8:58, cf. Col 2:9), therefore, *qualitatively*, He was God manifest in the flesh; while *quantitatively* speaking, He was limited as a man and could in all truthfulness state "My Father is greater than I." When this comparison of position in John 14:28 and the comparison of *nature* in Hebrews 1 are clearly understood, the argument Jehovah's Witnesses attempt to raise in order to rob Christ of His deity is reduced to rubble before one of the greatest of all truths revealed in Scripture, namely, that "God who made the world and all things therein" so loved us as to appear in our form (Jn 1:1, 14) that the sons of men might through His measureless grace, at length, become the sons of God.

We should be quick to recognize, however, that had the Lord Jesus said in John 14:28 that his Father was *better* than He was and had used the proper Greek word denoting this type of comparison, another issue would be involved, but in actuality, the comparison between Christ and His Father in that context and verse clearly indicates that Jesus was speaking as a man and not as the second Person of the Trinity (Jn 1:1). Therefore it is perfectly understandable that He should humble Himself before His Father and declare that in the present form in which He found Himself, His Father most certainly was "greater," positionally, than He. One might be willing to admit that the President of the United States is a *greater* man by virtue of his present position, authority, and recognition, but it would be a far different matter to assent to the proposition that the President of the United States is a *better* man than his fellow Americans in the sense of *quality*, because such a comparison then involves a discussion of fundamental natures and attributes. In like manner, then, Jesus as the incarnate Son of God, who had by His own voluntary act of will, divested Himself of His prerogatives of intrinsic deity, could speak of His Father as being *positionally* greater than He was without in any sense violating His true deity or humanity.

Hebrews 1:4 clearly teaches that Christ is better than the angels *qualitatively* from all eternity, and that even while He walked the earth, though He was made lower than the angels *positionally* for the suffering of death in the form of a man, never for an instant did He ever cease to be the Lord of glory who could say with confident assurance, "Before Abraham was I AM" (Jn 8:58, KJV).

Let us be constantly aware of these facts when discussing the nature of Christ with Jehovah's Witnesses, for once the distinction is made between "greater" and "better," their entire argument based upon John 14:28 melts into nothingness, and the deity of our Lord is completely vindicated by the whole testimony of Scripture.

Born again. Many times in their contacts with Christians, Jehovah's Witnesses utilize the evangelical terminology of the gospel of John, chapter 3, where Christ, speaking to Nicodemus, said, "Except a man be born again he cannot see the kingdom of God." The Witnesses utilize such terminology because they realize that contemporary evangelical efforts have popularized this term, and the Watchtower is quick to capitalize on any popularization of a biblical term, especially if it can be twisted to serve its own end! The definition which Jehovah's Witnesses give to the new birth or the act of being "born again" is found on page 48 of their text-book *Make Sure of All Things* and is as follows: "Born again means a birth-like realization of prospects and hopes for spirit life by resurrection to heaven. Such a realization is brought about through the water of God's truth in the Bible and God's holy spirit, his active force."

One can see from this definition that the Witnesses flatly reject the concept of the new birth as taught in the New Testament. The Bible teaches us that when we are born again, it is through repentance, the washing of water by the Word, and the direct agency of the third Person of the Trinity, God the Holy Spirit. (Jn 3; Eph 5:26; 1 Pe 1:23). There is not one verse that may be cited in either the Old or New Testaments to prove that the new birth means "a birth-like realization of prospects and hopes for spirit life by resurrection to heaven," as Jehovah's Witnesses so brazenly misrepresent it. On the contrary, the new birth guarantees eternal life to *all* believers, entrance into the kingdom of heaven, and a resurrection to immortality in a deathless, incorruptible form similar to that of the Lord Jesus Christ's form when He rose from among the dead.

The theology of Jehovah's Witnesses, relevant to the new birth, is that there will be only 144,000 "spiritual brothers" who will reign with Christ in heaven for a thousand years; and, further, that only these 144,000 will have a resurrection to heaven and a "spirit life," such as that now allegedly enjoyed by Pastor Charles Taze Russell and Judge J. F. Rutherford, who are carrying on the work of the Society "within the veil," according to Watchtower teaching.

In direct contrast to this, the Lord Jesus Christ made a universal statement when He stated, "Except a man be born again he cannot see the kingdom of God," and we find no record of either Christ, the disciples, or the apostles ever promulgating the 144,000 "spirit brothers" idea espoused so zealously by the Watchtower. A doctrine of such momentous importance, the authors feel, would certainly have been carefully defined in the New Testament; yet it is not, and the only support Jehovah's Witnesses can garner for this weird Russellite interpretation is from the book of Revelation and the mystical number "144,000" which, incidentally, the

Bible teaches, refers to the twelve tribes of Israel, twelve thousand out of each tribe, and therefore certainly *not* members of the Watchtower's theocracy.

Christians should therefore be on guard continually against the Watchtower's perversion of common biblical terms drawn from evangelical sources, for in 90 percent of the cases which the authors have analyzed, the Witnesses *mean* just the opposite of what they *appear* to say. The new birth, Peter tells us in the original Greek, is a *past* event in the lives of those who have experienced the regenerating power of God's Spirit (1 Pe 1:23); it is not something to be constantly experiencing or to be looking forward to in a type of ethereal spiritual resurrection, as the Witnesses would have us believe. Rather, it is a fact to be rejoiced in that we "have been born again" and are new creations in Christ Jesus (2 Co 5:17), joint heirs in the glory of the kingdom, which is yet to be revealed.

The Watchtower Bible and Tract Society most decidedly has its "new birth," but it is not the new birth of Scripture, nor is their theory taught anywhere within the pages of the Bible. It is instead the theological brainchild of Charles Taze Russell, to which the Witnesses cling so tenaciously, and which in the end will be found to have originated with "the god of this world" who has blinded their eyes "lest the glorious light of the gospel of Christ, who is the image of God should shine unto them."

Death. In common with other deviant systems of theology, Jehovah's Witnesses espouse a peculiar and definitely unbiblical concept of death, both in regard to the physical body and the soul and spirit of man.

According to the Watchtower publication, *Make Sure of All Things,* death is defined in the following manner: "Death—loss of life; termination of existence; utter cessation of conscious intellectual or physical activity, celestial, human, or otherwise" (p. 86).

Reverting to their basic trait of text-lifting and term-switching, Jehovah's Witnesses garner a handful of texts from the Old and New Testaments which speak of death as "sleep" or "unconsciousness," and from these out-of-context quotations, attempt to prove that at the death of the physical form, man, like the beasts, ceases to exist until the resurrection.

Seizing upon such texts as Psalm 13:3; Ecclesiastes 9:5-6, 10; and Daniel 12:2, the Witnesses loudly contend that until the resurrection, the dead remain unconscious and inactive in the grave, thus doing away in one fell swoop with the doctrine of hell and the true biblical teaching regarding the soul of man.

It is impossible in this short study to place all the verses Jehovah's Witnesses lift out of their contexts back into their proper contextual-hermeneutical position, and by so doing, show that their theory is an exegetical nightmare, but the following observation can be made:

Despite the fact that in the Old Testament the term *sleep* is used to denote death, never once is such a term used to describe the immaterial nature of man, which the Scriptures teach was created in the image of God (Gen 1:26-27). This fact also holds true in the New Testament, as any cursory study of either Strong's or Young's concordances will reveal. The term *sleep* is always applied to the body, since in death, the body takes on the appearance of one who is asleep, but the term *soul sleep* or *the sleep of the soul* is never found in Scripture, and nowhere does it state that the soul ever sleeps or passes into a state of unconsciousness. The only way that Jehovah's Witnesses can infer such a doctrine is by assuming beforehand that death *means* sleep or unconsciousness; hence, every time they are confronted with the term *death*, they assign the meaning of extinction of consciousness to it, and by so doing, remove from Scripture the doctrine which they fear and hate the most—that of conscious punishment after death for unregenerate souls, continuing on into the everlasting ages of eternity (2 Pe 2:17; Jude 10-13).

Since we have already covered the doctrine of hell in a previous chapter, the simplest refutation of Jehovah's Witnesses perverted terms, such as *death*, can be found in the Scriptures themselves, where it can easily be shown that death does not mean "termination of existence"; "utter cessation of conscious intellectual . . . activity," as the Watchtower desperately attempts to establish.

Note the following references: John 11:26; Romans 8:10; Ephesians 2:1-5; and Philippians 1:21. The usage of *death* in these passages clearly indicates a state of existence solely in opposition to the definition which the Watchtower assigns to the word *death,* and the reader need only substitute the Watchtower's definition in each one of these previously enumerated passages to see how utterly absurd it is to believe that the body has experienced "the loss of life" or "termination of existence" in such a context where Paul writes, "If Christ be in you, the body is dead because of sin" (Ro 8:10, KJV). The inspired apostle here obviously refers to a spiritual condition of separation—certainly not to "termination of existence," as the Watchtower's definition states.

We see, therefore, that death is a separation of the soul and spirit *from* the body, resulting in physical inactivity and a general *appearance* of sleep; however, in the spiritual sense, death is the separation of soul and spirit from God as the result of sin, and in no sense of the term can it ever be honestly translated "unconsciousness" or "termination of existence," as Jehovah's Witnesses would like to have it.

In his epistle to the Thessalonians, the fourth chapter, the apostle Paul spoke of the return of the Lord Jesus Christ and most pointedly made use of the term *sleep* as a metaphor for death (1 Th 4:13-18), and it is interesting to note his concept: "But I would not have you to be ignorant, brethren, concerning them which are asleep, that ye sorrow not, even as others which have no hope. For if we believe that Jesus died and rose again, even so them also which sleep in Jesus will God bring *with* him. For this we say unto you by the word of the Lord, that we which are alive and remain unto the coming of the Lord shall not prevent them which are asleep. For the Lord himself shall descend from heaven with a shout, with the voice of the archangel, and with the trump of God: and the dead in Christ shall rise first: Then we which are alive and remain shall be caught up together with them in the clouds, to meet the Lord in the air: and so shall we ever be with the Lord. Wherefore comfort one another with these words" (KJV).

Verse 14 of this previously quoted section indicates that Paul, while using the metaphor *sleep* to describe physical death, clearly understood that when Jesus comes again, He will bring *with* (*sun,* Greek) Him those whose bodies are sleeping. To be more explicit, the souls and spirits of those who are with Christ now in glory (2 Co 5:8; Phil 1:22-23) will be reunited with their resurrection bodies (1 Co 15); that is, they will be clothed with immortality, incorruptibility, exemption from physical decay, and they will be coming *with* Jesus. The Greek *sun* indicates in a "side by side" position, and the bodies that are sleeping will in that instant, be quickened, raised to immortality, and reunited with the perfected spirits of the returning saints.

This passage alone would be enough to convince any exegetical scholar that those "sleeping in Jesus" must refer to their *bodies*, since they are in the same verse spoken of as coming *with* Jesus, and by no possible stretch of the imagination could one honestly exegete the passage so as to teach anything to the contrary.

Jehovah's Witnesses are deathly afraid of the "everlasting fire" prepared for the devil and his followers (Mt 25:41), and their entire system of theology is dedicated to a contradiction of this important biblical teaching of God's eternal wrath upon those who perpetrate the infinite transgressions of denying His beloved Son. Rightly, then, does the Bible say that "The wrath of God continues to abide upon them" (Jn 3:36), for they have merited eternal judgment and "contempt" which they, along with their master, Satan, will receive at the great and terrible day of the Lord (Dan 12:2; Mark 9:43, 48; Rev 20:10).

For the Christian, then, physical death involves only the sleep of the body, pending the resurrection to immortality, when our resurrection bodies will be joined to our perfected souls and spirits; but in the intermediate state, should we die before the Lord comes, we have the assurance that we shall be *with Him* and that we shall return *with Him*, or as the apostle Paul stated it, "To be absent from the body is to be at home (or present) with the Lord."

The preceding information is offered as proof that, contrary to the teachings of Jehovah's Witnesses, death does not mean "termination of existence" but rather the separation of the soul and spirit from the physical form, the unsaved going to hell and later to eternal judgment, while the souls of the saints go to be "forever with the Lord."

Firstborn (*prototokos*, Greek). The authors feel it necessary to include a brief resumé of Jehovah's Witnesses misuse of the Greek term *prototokos* (Col 1:15), which the Watchtower lays much emphasis upon, since it is used descriptively of the Lord Jesus Christ; and so in their Arian theology, it is construed to teach that Christ is the first creature, since the word "firstborn" implies that of the *first* child.

In Colossians 1, the apostle Paul speaks of the Lord Jesus Christ as the firstborn of every creature, or of all creation. And the Witnesses, always eager to reduce Christ to the rank of an angel, have seized upon these passages of Scripture as indicative of His creaturehood. The Watchtower teaches that since Christ is called the "first born of all creation," therefore He must be the *first one* created, and they cross-reference this with Revelation 3:14, which states that the faithful and true witness (Christ) is "the beginning of the creation of God."

On the surface, the argument the Watchtower erects appears to be fairly sound, but underneath it, it is found to be both shallow and fraudulent. The term firstborn (*prototokos*) may also rightfully be rendered "first begetter" or "original bringer forth" (Erasmus), a term of preeminence, and in Colossians 1 it is a term of comparison between Christ and created *things*. In the first chapter of Colossians, Paul points out that Christ is "before all things" and clearly establishes the fact that the eternal Word of God (Jn 1:1) existed before all creation (Heb 1), that He is preeminent over all creation, by virtue of the fact that He is Deity; and beyond this, that He is the Creator of all "things," which to any rational person indicates that if He is Creator of all things, He Himself is not created! In the eighth chapter of Romans, verse 29, the word *firstborn* is applied to Christ, clearly denoting His preeminence—not the concept that He is, "the first creature made by Jehovah God," as the Witnesses would like us to believe, and in Colossians 1:18, we learn that Christ is "firstborn" from the dead, that is, the first one to rise in a resurrection body. Again the meaning is that of preeminence, not of creation.‡

"The beginning of the creation of God" (Rev 3:14) is easily

‡A careful analysis of the Septuagint usage of *firstborn* also forcibly refutes the Watchtower. In Genesis 41:51-52, Manasseh is called God's "firstborn," but in Jeremiah 31:9, Ephraim replaces him as "firstborn," or "preeminent one" because of Manasseh's sins. Clearly, *firstborn* does not always mean "the first one born," as Jehovah's witnesses teach.

harmonized with the rest of Scripture which teaches the absolute deity of the Lord Jesus Christ, when we realize that the Greek word *arche*, which is translated "beginning," is translated by the Witnesses themselves as "originally" in John 1:1 of their own *New World Translation*—and this is a good translation at this point—so applying it to Revelation 3:14, Christ becomes the "origin" or the "source" of the creation of God (Knox), and not the very beginning of it Himself, in the sense that He is the *first* creation, a fact which Scripture most pointedly contradicts.

Christ is therefore "firstborn" or preeminent by virtue of the fact that He is Deity, and by virtue of the fact that He is the first one to rise in a glorified body. He is therefore preeminent over all creation, and through His power all things consist or hold together. He is not one of the "things" (Col 1:16-17) but He is the Creator of *all* things, the eternal Word who possesses the very nature of God (Heb 1:3).

Soul and spirit (psuche, pneuma, Greek). Jehovah's Witnesses delight in the assertion that man does not possess an immaterial, deathless nature,§ and they never tire of proclaiming such teaching to be "a lie of the devil" and a dogma derived from pagan religions (Egyptian, Babylonian, Greek). The literature of Jehovah's Witnesses is filled with condemnations of the doctrine of the immaterial nature of man, which the authors took up in chapter 4. According to the Watchtower, the soul is "a living, breathing, sentient creature, animal or human," and Jehovah's Witnesses also define a spirit as "a life force, or something wind-like."[4]

By so defining these two, common, biblical terms, the Watchtower seeks to avoid the embarrassing scriptural truth that since man is created in the image of God and God is Spirit, man must possess a cognizant spiritual entity formed in the image of his Creator (Gen 1:26-27). To explode this Watchtower mythology is an elementary task, when we realize that when the Lord Jesus Christ died upon the cross, He said, "Father, into thy hands I commend my spirit," a fact Jehovah's Witnesses are hard put to explain, since, if the spirit is nothing but breath or wind, and

§In the sense of extinction that is, for the soul is spoken of as being extinct or unconscious.

certainly not a conscious entity, as the Bible teaches it is, then it would be fruitless for Christ to commit His breath to the Father; yet He did precisely that! The truth of the matter is that the Lord Jesus Christ committed to His Father His immaterial nature as a man, proving conclusively that the spirit and soul of man goes into eternity as a conscious entity (Gal 6:8).

It will also be remembered that when Stephen was stoned, he fell asleep in death, but not before he said, "Lord Jesus, receive my spirit," and in that particular context, it is rather obvious that he was not referring to the exhalation of carbon dioxide from his lungs! However, we may safely say that the meanings Jehovah's Witnesses give to *soul* and *spirit* will not stand the test of systematic exegesis in either the Old or New Testament, and no competent Hebrew or Greek scholar today has ever espoused their cause in open scholastic discussion.

Wisdom. Jehovah's Witnesses constantly carp on the fact that Jesus Christ is called the wisdom of God (1 Co 1) and that in Proverbs 8 wisdom is said to have been created by Jehovah; therefore, Christ is a created being. This bit of word juggling falls flat when one observes that the same wisdom is called by the *female* gender (Pr 8:1-3; 9:1-4), hardly applicable to a male Messiah! Moreover, Christ is not even mentioned in Proverbs 8, except by deduction. Every first year Hebrew student recognizes this as the common literary device of personification, or the attributing of personality to an object or concept.

Concluding this synopsis of the misapplications and misinterpretations of Jehovah's Witnesses, where biblical terms and texts are concerned, the authors feel constrained to state that by no means have we thoroughly covered this vast subject.

Jehovah's Witnesses thrive on the confusion they are able to create, and in their door-to-door canvassing, they accentuate this trait by demonstrating extreme reluctance to identify themselves as emissaries of the Watchtower until they have established a favorable contact with the prospective convert. To put it in the terms of the vernacular, until they have "made the pitch," they are careful to conceal their identity. To illustrate this particular point more fully, the *New Yorker* magazine, June 16, 1956, carried a lengthy article by one of its feature writers (at that time), Richard Harris, in which Mr. Harris recounts his experiences with Jehovah's Witnesses. In this article, Mr. Harris relates that the Witnesses never identified themselves to prospective converts as Jehovah's Witnesses at first when Mr. Harris accompanied a team of Witnesses on one of their daily canvassing routes in Brooklyn. Mr. Harris also pointed out in the article that the Witnesses openly admitted to him that it was necessary for them first to make a successful contact before they fully identified themselves. In short, they fly under false colors: "A representative of Radio Station WBBR," "A Bible student," or "a minister," but seldom if ever as a Jehovah's Witness.

The late Judge J. F. Rutherford has well taught his followers to "Advertise, advertise, advertise!" And today throughout the world, Jehovah's Witnesses are advertising, advertising, and selling, selling, the theocracy of Charles Taze Russell and J. F. Rutherford under any label that is convenient, and that will gain for them a hearing.

If evangelical Christianity continues to virtually ignore today the activities of Jehovah's Witnesses, it does so at the peril of countless souls. Therefore, let us awaken to their perversions of Scripture and stand fast in the defense of the faith "once delivered unto the saints."

Nowhere is this point more forcefully demonstrated than in a book authored by a former member of the Watchtower Society, W. J. Schnell. In this particular reference, Schnell succinctly states the Watch Tower methodology in the following words:

> The Watch Tower leadership sensed that within the midst of Christendom were many millions of professing Christians who were not well grounded in "the truths once delivered to the saints," and who would be rather easily pried loose from the churches and led into a new and revitalized Watch Tower organization. The Society calculated, and that rightly, that this lack of proper knowledge of God and the widespread acceptance of half-truths in Christendom would yield vast masses of men and women, if the whole matter were wisely attacked, the attack sustained and the results contained, and then re-used in an ever-widening circle.[5]

The end product of this whole cult is the denial of the Lord Jesus Christ as "very God of very God," and despite their protests that they honor Christ, they do indeed dishonor and "crucify him afresh," since they deny His deity and Lordship. Regardless of their biblical names and proficiency in the Scriptures, they constantly reveal their true character in their actions, which are the diametric opposite of scriptural teachings. The following old adage is most appropriate in describing the doctrines of Jehovah's Witnesses: "No matter how you label it or what color bottle you put it in, poison is still poison." "He that hath ears to hear, let him hear."

There can be no kingdom without the King, however, and His return is visible, with power and glory (Mt 24:30); their kingdom has come (1914-18), but with no visible king, power, or glory. Jehovah of the Watchtower is a conjectural myth, a creation of the reactionary theology of Charles Taze Russell, and is conformed to the pattern of Russell's mind and education, which continued through Rutherford and now continues through Knorr to the ever increasing blindness of those misguided souls foolish enough to trust in the Russellite delusion. In comparison to the Scriptures, this picture is infinite darkness, for its author is the "prince of darkness," and the Word of God clearly and incontestably reveals that "Jehovah of the Watchtower" is not the Jehovah of the Bible, for Jehovah of the Bible is Lord of all— "The great God and our Saviour Jesus Christ" (Titus 2:13, KJV).

Appendix

THE FOLLOWING documented information reveals most adequately just how reliable the Watchtower is in matters of biblical prophecy.

1. If the reader will study the excerpts taken from a famous trial in Scotland, involving the Watchtower and its New World Translation, some amazing facts emerge. F. W. Franz, vice-president of the Watchtower Society, swore he was competent to read and therefore translate Hebrew, and as a member of the New World Translation committee, he should have been. Here is an excerpt from that court transcript.

> Q: Have you also made yourself familiar with Hebrew? A: Yes.
> Q: So that you have a substantial linguistic apparatus at your command? A: Yes, for use in my biblical work. Q: I think you are able to read and follow the Bible in Hebrew, Greek, Latin, Spanish, Portuguese, German, and French? A: Yes.*

The truth is that F. W. Franz holds no degree in Greek or Hebrew, and cannot read either Greek or Hebrew, as a translator should. He dropped out of the University of Cincinnati after his sophomore year and had not been studying anything having to do with theology. Therefore, his qualifications as the only officially recognized member of the translation committee are definitely not adequate. Later, during the same crossexamination, Franz had to admit that he was unable to translate a Bible verse:

> Q: You, yourself, read and speak Hebrew, do you? A: I do not speak Hebrew. Q: You do not? A: No. Q: Can you, yourself translate that into Hebrew? A: Which? Q: That fourth verse of the second chapter of Genesis? A: You mean here? Q: Yes. A: No.†

*This information is from the Pursuer's Proof of the crossexamination held on Wednesday, November 24, 1954, p. 7, pars. A—B.
†Ibid., p. 102, par. F.

2. The following paragraph is an excerpt from Dr. Mantey's letter of February 25, 1974, to Mr. Van Buskirk, which is referred to in chapter 3, page 51 of this book.

"In Jehovah's Witnesses translation of the New Testament where I am quoted in a footnote on Jn 1:1 (cf. D-M, *Greek Grammar,* p. 148), I was writing on how *the article* 'distinguishes the subject from the predicate in a copulative sentence,' not on the significance of the absence of the article before *theos.* My closing statement in the paragraph was: 'As it stands, the other persons of the Trinity may be implied in *theos.*' My interpretation of Jn 1:1 in that same paragraph was 'The word was deity,' i.e., that Christ is of the same essence as the Father, of the same family. So I was quoted out of context. Is that honest scholarship?"

3. The five known members of New World Translation committee, discussed in chapter 8, page 129 of this book, are as follows: chairman, Nathan H. Knorr; Fred W. Franz; George D. Gangos; Milton G. Herschell; and A. D. Schroeder. With the exception of F. W. Franz, none of the committee attended college, and he dropped out of the University of Cincinnati after his second year.

None of the committee members reads New Testament Greek or, for that matter, Hebrew or Aramaic. They "translated" a text they could not read. In the words of the late Dr. Edgar Goodspeed, a Greek and Hebrew scholar whose endorsement they sought and were refused, "Their grammar is regrettable."

4. In the November 1, 1972, issue of *The Watchtower,* the society made the following contradictory statement: "Does their admission of making mistakes stamp them as false prophets? *Not at all,* for false prophets do not admit making mistakes" (*Watchtower,* Nov. 1, 1972).

The Bible defines a false prophet as someone who utters prophecies that fail or mislead in fulfillment and in whom there is no light or, literally, "no dawn" (Is 8:20, NASB).

The following list of dates and prophecies was graciously compiled by the author's friend and co-worker, William Cetnar, a former Jehovah's Witness.

1889—"The 'battle of the great day of God Almighty' (Rev. 16:14), which will end in A.D. 1914 with the complete overthrow of earth's present rulership is already commenced" (*The Time Is at Hand,* p. 101).

1916—"The Bible chronology herein presented shows that the six great 1000-year days beginning with Adam are ended, and that the great 7th Day, the 1000 years of Christ's Reign, began in 1873" (*The Time Is at Hand,* p. 2 of the foreword).

1918—"Therefore we may confidently expect that 1925 will mark the return of Abraham, Isaac, Jacob and the faithful prophets of old, particularly those named by the Apostle in Hebrews chapter 11, to the condition of human perfection" (*Millions Now Living Will Never Die,* p. 89).

1922—"The date 1925 is even more distinctly indicated by the Scriptures than 1914" (*Watchtower,* Sept. 1, 1922, p. 262).

1923—"Our thought is, that 1925 is definitely settled by the Scriptures. As to Noah, the Christian now has much more upon which to base his faith in a coming deluge" (*Watchtower,* Apr. 1, 1923, p. 106).

1925—(January) "The year 1925 is here. With great expectation Christians have looked forward to this year. Many have confidently expected that all members of the body of Christ will be changed to heavenly glory during this year. This may be accomplished. It may not be. In his own due time God will accomplish his purposes concerning his people. Christians should not be so deeply concerned about what may transpire this year" (*Watchtower,* Jan. 1, 1925, p. 3).

1925—(September) "It is to be expected that Satan will try to inject into the minds of the consecrated the thought that 1925 should see an end to the work" (*Watchtower,* Sept. 1, 1925, p. 262).

1926—"Some anticipated that the work would end in 1925, but the Lord did not state so. The difficulty was that the friends inflated their imaginations beyond reason; and that when their imaginations burst asunder, they were inclined to throw away everything" (*Watchtower,* p. 232).

1931—"There was a measure of disappointment on the part of Jehovah's faithful ones on earth concerning the years 1914, 1918, and 1925, which disappointment lasted for a time . . .

and they also learned to quit fixing dates" (*Vindication*, p. 238).

1941—"Receiving the gift, the marching children clasped it to them, not a toy or plaything for idle pleasure, but the Lord's provided instrument for most effective work in the remaining months before Armageddon" (*Watchtower*, Sept. 15, 1941, p. 288).

1968—"True, there have been those in times past who predicted an 'end' to the world, even announcing a specific date. Yet nothing happened. The 'end' did not come. They were guilty of false prophesying. Why? What was missing? Missing from such people were God's truths and the evidence that he was using and guiding them" (*Awake*, Oct. 8, 1968). See Luke 21:8.

5. H. C. Covington, a former vice-president of the Watchtower board and a gifted lawyer, swore at the same trial where F. W. Franz testified, that the Watchtower was guilty of circulating false prophecies concerning the second coming of Christ. The following excerpt is taken from his testimony.‡

> Q: You have promulgated—forgive the word—false prophecy?
> A: We have. I do not think we have promulgated false prophecy. There have been statements that were erroneous, that is the way I put it, and mistaken.

He further testified that if a good Jehovah's Witness denounced these false prophecies, he would be disfellowshipped and considered worthy of death, even though he or she was right and the Society was wrong!

May we who are indwelled by the Holy Spirit pray for those who have been drawn into believing the fabrications of such people who draw nigh to God with their lips but whose hearts are far from Him.

‡Ibid., p. 340, par. *C*.

Notes

CHAPTER 1

1. Rev. J. J. Ross, *Some facts About the Self-styled "Pastor" Charles T. Russell*, p. 7.
2. Ibid., pp. 3-4.
3. J. J. Ross, *Some Facts and More Facts About the Self-styled Pastor—Charles T. Russell*, p. 15.
4. Ibid., p. 18.
5. Ibid., p. 17.
6. Ibid.
7. Ibid.
8. See J. F. Rutherford, *The Kingdom*, p. 14.
9. Rutherford, *Why Serve Jehovah?*, p. 62.
10. Rutherford, *Religious Intolerance—Why?*, p. 41.
11. Rutherford, *Jehovah's Witnesses—Why Persecuted?*, p. 41.

CHAPTER 2

1. J. F. Rutherford, *"Let God Be True,"* p. 81.
2. Ibid., p. 82.
3. Ibid., p. 87.
4. Ibid., p. 88.
5. Ibid., p. 91.
6. Ibid., pp. 91-92.
7. Ibid., p. 92.
8. Ibid., p. 93.
9. Ibid., p. 89.
10. Rutherford, *Harp of God*, pp. 102, 129.
11. Charles T. Russell, *Studies in the Scriptures*, vol. 5, *At-One-Ment Between God and Man*, p. 84.
12. Ibid., pp. 55, 84, 134.
13. Ibid., pp. 54, 60.
14. Ibid., p. 169.
15. Ibid., p. 210.
16. Rutherford, *Reconciliation*, p. 115, also, *"Let God Be True,"* p. 81.
17. Russell, *Studies in the Scriptures*, vol. 7, *Finished Mystery*, p. 414
18. Rutherford, *"Let God Be True,"* p. 272.
19. Russell, *At-One-Ment Between God and Man*, pp. 453-54.
20. Russell, *Studies in the Scriptures*, vol. 2, *The Time Is at Hand*, p. 129.
21. Rutherford, *"Let God Be True,"* p. 122.
22. Rutherford, *Harp of God*, p. 172.
23. Russell, *Studies in the Scriptures*, vol. 1, *Plan of the Ages*, p. 150.
24. Rutherford, *"Let God Be True,"* p. 96.
25. Ibid., p. 185.
26. Ibid., p. 186.

27. Ibid., pp. 187-88.
28. Ibid., p. 234.
29. Ibid., p. 235.
30. Ibid.
31. Ibid., p. 236.
32. Ibid., p. 68.
33. Ibid., pp. 72-73.
34. Ibid., p. 79.
35. Ibid.
36. Ibid., p. 80.
37. Rutherford, *World Distress*, p. 40.
38. Rutherford, *"Let God Be True,"* p. 47.
39. Ibid., p. 48.
40. Ibid., p. 55.
41. Ibid., pp. 55-56.
42. Ibid., p. 56.
43. Ibid., p. 59.
44. Ibid., pp. 59-60.
45. Ibid., p. 61.
46. Ibid., p. 63.
47. Ibid., p. 66.
48. Ibid., p. 67.
49. Ibid.
50. Ibid.
51. Ibid., p. 121.
52. Ibid., p. 122.
53. Ibid., pp. 122-23.
54. Ibid., pp. 123-24.
55. Ibid., p. 128.
56. Ibid.
57. Ibid., p. 129.
58. Russell, *At-One-Ment Between God and Man*, p. 166.
59. *The Truth Shall Make You Free*, p. 45.
60. Russell, *At-One-Ment Between God and Man*, p. 166.
61. *The Kingdom Is at Hand*, p. 507.
62. Russell, *At-One-Ment Between God and Man*, p. 166.
63. Rutherford, *"Let God Be True,"* p. 82.
64. Russell, *At-One-Ment Between God and Man*, p. 166.
65. Ibid., p. 55.
66. *The Truth Shall Make You Free*, p. 47.
67. Russell, *At-One-Ment Between God and Man*, p. 84.
68. *The Kingdom Is at Hand*, pp. 46-47, 49.
69. Russell, *At-One-Ment Between God and Man*, p. 86.
70. Rutherford, *"Let God Be True,"* pp. 34-35.
71. Russell, *At-One-Ment Between God and Man*, p. 84.
72. *The Truth Shall Make You Free*, p. 49.
73. Russell, *At-One-Ment Between God and Man*, p. 453.
74. *The Kingdom Is at Hand*, p. 258.
75. Russell, *At-One-Ment Between God and Man*, p. 454.
76. Rutherford, *"Let God Be True,"* pp. 43, 122.
77. Russell, *The Time Is at Hand*, p. 127.
78. *The Kingdom Is at Hand*, p. 259.
79. Russell, *The Time Is at Hand*, p. 129.
80. Rutherford, *"Let God Be True,"* p. 185.
81. Russell, *The Time Is at Hand*, p. 154.
82. Rutherford, *"Let God Be True,"* p. 185.
83. Russell, *The Time Is at Hand*, p. 191.

84. Rutherford, *"Let God Be True,"* p. 186.
85. Russell, *The Time Is at Hand,* p. 108.
86. *The Truth Shall Make You Free,* pp. 295, 300.
87. Russell, *Plan of the Ages,* p. 127.
88. Rutherford, *"Let God Be True,"* p. 72.
89. Russell, *Plan of the Ages,* p. 128.
90. Rutherford, *"Let God Be True,"* pp. 79, 80.

CHAPTER 3

1. J. F. Rutherford, *"Let God Be True,"* p. 81.
2. Ibid., p. 82.
3. Ibid., pp. 81-93.
4. See *The Truth Shall Make You Free,* p. 47.
5. Brown, Francis; Driver, S. R.; and Briggs, Charles A., *Hebrew and English Lexicon of the Old Testament,* p. 426a, Item 2.
6. *New World Translation of the Christian Greek Scriptures,* pp. 773-77, remarks on Appendix note to Jn 1:1.
7. Ibid., p. 776b.
8. A. T. Robertson, quoted in NWT, p. 755.
9. NWT, p. 312, n. c.
10. Ibid., p. 880.
11. Joseph Henry Thayer, *A Greek-English Lexicon of the New Testament,* p. 288.
12. Ibid.
13. Rutherford, p. 88.

CHAPTER 4

1. Russell, Charles T., *The Time Is at Hand,* p. 129. Russell also stated that "the man Jesus is dead, forever dead" (*At-One-Ment Between God and Man,* p. 454), a view directly refuted by the apostle Paul in 1 Ti 2:5, where he calls Christ "the mediator" thirty years after the resurrection, and He mediates as a man.
2. *The Truth Shall Make You Free,* p. 295.
3. J. H. Thayer, *Greek-English Lexicon of the New Testament,* p. 490.
4. Ibid., p. 648.
5. J. F. Rutherford, *"Let God Be True,"* p. 77.
6. Thayer, p. 96b.
7. Rutherford, p. 74.
8. Ibid., p. 79.
9. Ibid., p. 56.
10. See James Strong's *Exhaustive Concordance of the Bible,* p. 11. The Hebrew letters are *Aleph* (*A*), *Yod* (*Y*), *Nun* (*N*), transliterated *AYIN.*

CHAPTER 5

1. See *Awake,* May 22, 1951, p. 4.
2. Ibid., p. 6.
3. *Awake,* Jan. 22, 1952, p. 160.
4. *Chicago Herald Almanac,* Apr. 18, 1951.
5. *The Watchtower,* July 1, 1951, p. 415.
6. *Awake,* Feb. 22, 1951.
7. J. F. Rutherford, "Children of the King," radio address.

CHAPTER 6

1. Stanley High, "Armageddon, Inc.," *Saturday Evening Post*, June 1940.
2. "Showing Concern For the Poor," *The Watchtower*, Dec. 1951, pp. 731-33.
3. Ibid., p. 731.
4. Ibid.
5. Ibid., p. 732.
6. Ibid.
7. Ibid., pp. 732-33.
8. Ibid., p. 733.
9. Ibid. Emphasis added.
10. "Jehovah a Strong Refuge Today," *The Watchtower*, October 1, 1952, pp. 596-604.
11. Ibid., p. 601.
12. Ibid., p. 599.
13. J. F. Rutherford, *Reconciliation*, pp. 85, 91, 100, 101, and 125.
14. Ibid.

CHAPTER 7

1. C. T. Russell, *The Plan of the Ages*, p. 41.
2. "The Scriptures, Reason, and the Trinity," *The Watchtower*, January 1, 1953, p. 22.
3. Ibid., p. 24.
4. Ibid., p. 24.
5. Ibid.
6. Ibid.
7. Ibid.
8. J. H. Thayer, *Greek-English Lexicon of the New Testament*, p. 307
9. "The Scriptures, Reason, and the Trinity," p. 22.

CHAPTER 8

1. *Make Sure of All Things*, p. 319. (*Make Sure of All Things* is a compilation of Scriptures, arranged under various subjects with some explanatory comments. No author's name is given.)
2. Ibid., pp. 319, 320-23.
3. J. H. Thayer, *A Greek-English Lexicon of the New Testament*, p. 490.

CHAPTER 9

1. "Are You Born Again?" *Awake* (June 22, 1955), pp. 9-11. This title is, of course, very misleading, for the Witnesses deny the personality of the Holy Spirit, through whose power alone one may be "born again."
2. Ibid., p. 10.
3. Ibid., p. 11.
4. NWT, quoted in *Awake*, p. 9.
5. Ibid.
6. Ibid.

CHAPTER 10

1. H. G. Liddell and R. Scott, *A Greek-English Lexicon*, 2:1144.
2. James Hope Moulton and George Milligan, *The Vocabulary of the Greek Testament*, pp. 416-17.
3. J. H. Thayer, *Greek-English Lexicon of the New Testament*, p. 417
4. *Make Sure of All Things*, p. 357.
5. W. J. Schnell, *Thirty Years a Watchtower Slave*, p. 19.

Bibliography

GENERAL SOURCES

Carnall, E. J. *An Introduction to Christian Apologetics.* Grand Rapids: Eerdmans, 1950.

Cole, Marley. *Jehovah's Witnesses—The New World Society.* New York: Vantage, 1955.

Conner, W. T. *The Teachings of "Pastor" Russell.* Nashville: Southern Baptist, 1926.

Cooksey, N. B. *Russellism Under the Searchlight.*

Davies, Horton. *Christian Deviations.* Philosophical Library.

Deissman, Adolf. *Light from the Ancient East.* New York: Harper, 1951.

Dencher, Ted. *The Watch Tower Versus the Bible.* Chicago: Moody, 1961.

Finegan, Jack. *Light from the Ancient Past.* Princeton: Princeton U., 1946.

Gaebelein, Arno C. *The Hope of the Ages.* New York: Our Hope, 1938.

Gaebelein, Frank E. *Exploring the Bible.* Wheaton, Ill.: Van Kampen, 1950.

Haldeman, I. M. *A Great Counterfeit.* New York, n.d.

Hamilton, Floyd E. *The Basis of Christian Faith.* New York: Harper, 1949.

Irvine, William C. *Heresies Exposed.* New York: Loizeaux, 1955.

Machen, J. G. *The Origin of Paul's Religion.* Grand Rapids: Eerdmans, 1950.

———. *The Virgin Birth of Christ.* Grand Rapids: Eerdmans, 1950.

MacMillan, A. H. *Faith on the March.* Englewood Cliffs, N. J.: Prentice-Hall, 1957.

Mead, Frank S. *Handbook of the Denominations.* Nashville, Tenn.: Abingdon, 1951.

Newman, John Henry. *The Arians of the Fourth Century.* New York: Longmans, 1911.

———. *St. Athanasius.* Vols. 1 & 2. New York: Random, 1950.

Pegis, Anton C. *Basic Writings of St. Augustine.* New York: Random, 1950.

——. *Basic Writings of St. Thomas Aquinas.* New York: Random, 1950.

Ross, Rev. J. J. *Some Facts About the Self-styled Pastor, Charles T. Russell.* New York: Charles C. Cook, n.d.

——. *Some Facts and More Facts About the Self-styled Pastor, Charles T. Russell.* New York: Charles C. Cook, n.d.

Sanders, J. Oswald. *Heresies Ancient and Modern.* Edinburgh: Marshall, Morgan & Scott, 1954.

Schnell, W. J. *Thirty Years a Watch Tower Slave.* Grand Rapids: Baker, 1956.

——. *Into the Light of Christianity.* Grand Rapids: Baker, 1958.

Thiessen, Henry. *An Introduction to the New Testament.* Grand Rapids: Eerdmans, 1948.

Warfield, Benjamin B. *Christological Studies.* Princeton: Princeton U., 1950.

Wilson, Robert Dick. *A Scientific Investigation of the Old Testament.* Philadelphia: Sunday School Times, 1926.

Wright, J. Stafford. *Some Modern Religions.* Chicago: IVP, 1956.

Wulfken, George W. *Let There Be Light.* 1960.

Young, E. J. *An Introduction to the Old Testament.* 2d. ed. Grand Rapids: Eerdmans, 1950.

REFERENCE WORKS

Arndt, W. F. and Gingrich, F. W., ed. and trans. *Greek-English Lexicon of the New Testament and Other Early Christian Literature.* Chicago: U. of Chicago, 1957.

Ball, Frances K. *The Elements of Greek.* New York: Macmillan, 1948.

Brown, Francis; Driver, S. R.; and Briggs, Charles A. *Hebrew and English Lexicon of the Old Testament.* New York: Houghton-Mifflin, 1907.

Bullions, Peter. *Principles of Greek Grammar.* New York: Farmer, Bruce, n.d.

Cruden, Alexander. *Cruden's Complete Concordance.* Grand Rapids: Zondervan, 1949.

The Emphatic Diaglott. New York: Fowler & Wells, 1892.

The Englishman's Greek Concordance and the New Testament. London: Samuel Bagster, n.d.

Goodwin, W. W. *Syntax of the Moods and Tenses of the Greek Verb.* Boston: Ginn, 1900.

The Greek New Testament from the Text of Tischendorf. London: Elliot Stock, n.d.

The Hebrew Bible—The Old Testament According to Jewish Enumeration.

Knoch, Adolf E.; ed. *The Sacred Scriptures, Concordant Version* (New Testament). Los Angeles: Concordant, 1931.

Knox, Ronald. *Translation of the Bible.* 3 vols. New York: Sheed & Ward, 1953.

Liddell, Henry George; and Scott, Robert. *A Greek-English Lexicon.* 7th ed. rev. New York: Harper, 1883.

Moulton, J. H. *A Grammar of New Testament Greek.* 3d. ed. Edinburgh: T. & T. Clark, 1908.

Moulton, James Hope; and Milligan, George. *The Vocabulary of the Greek Testament.* Reprint. London: Hodder & Stoughton, 1952.

Nestle, D. E. *The New Testament in Greek.* Stuttgart, Germany: Privileg. Württ. Bibleanstalt, n.d.

Robertson, A. T. *A Grammar of the Greek New Testament in the Light of History.* London: Hodder & Stoughton, 1914.

The Septuagint Translation. Vols. 1 & 2. Stuttgart, Germany, 1949 (LXX).

Souter, Alexander. *The New Testament in Greek.* New York: Oxford, 1947.

Strong, James. *The Exhaustive Concordance of the Bible.* New York: Eaton & Mains, 1890.

Thayer, Joseph Henry. *Greek-English Lexicon of the New Testament.* Reprint. Grand Rapids: Zondervan, 1956.

Westcott, Brooke Foss; and Hort, John Fenton Anthony. *The New Testament in the Original Greek.* New York: Macmillan, 1885.

———. *The New Testament in the Original Greek.* Reprint. New York: Macmillan, 1943.

Yonge, C. D. *An English-Greek Lexicon.* London, 1959.

Young, G. Douglas. *Grammar of the Hebrew Language.* Grand Rapids: Zondervan, 1951.

Young, Robert. *Analytical Concordance to the Bible.* New York: Funk & Wagnalls, 1919.

MAGAZINE AND NEWSPAPER ARTICLES

The Brooklyn Daily Eagle, 1912, 1913, 1916.
The Brooklyn Daily Times, November 1, 1916.
The Brooklyn Eagle, 1942.
The Daily Standard Union, November 1, 1916.
Davidson, Bill. "Jehovah's Travelling Salesmen." *Readers Digest.* February, 1947.

High, Stanley. "Armageddon, Inc.," *Saturday Evening Post*, June 1940.

The New York Times, 1916.

Stewart, E. D. "The Life of Charles Taze Russell." *Overland Monthly.* 1917.

MISCELLANEOUS

The following books and other publications, all published by the Watchtower Bible and Tract Society, were read in preparation for this book. We do not endorse them for general reading.

Awake, assorted copies.

The Emphatic Diaglott, Interlinear Greek-English Translation of the New Testament.

Equipped for Every Good Work.

The Kingdom Is at Hand.

Knorr, N. H. *Can You Live Forever in Happiness on Earth?*

Make Sure of All Things. 1953.

A New Heaven and a New Earth. 1953.

The New World Translation of the Christian Greek Scriptures. 1950.

The New World Translation of the Christian Greek Scriptures. Rev. ed. 1951.

The New World Translation of the Hebrew Scriptures. Vols. 1 & 2. 1953 & 1955.

Qualified to Be Ministers. 1955.

Russell, Charles T. *Studies in the Scriptures.* Vol. 1, *The Plan of the Ages.* 1886.

——. *Studies in the Scriptures.* Vol. 2. *The Time Is at Hand.* 1907.

——. *Studies in the Scriptures.* Vol. 3. *Thy Kingdom Come.* 1910.

——. *Studies in the Scriptures.* Vol. 4. *The Battle of Armageddon.* 1910.

——. *Studies in the Scriptures.* Vol. 5. *The At-One-Ment Between God and Man.*

——. *Studies in the Scriptures.* Vol. 6. *The New Creation.* 1904

——. *Studies in the Scriptures.* Vol. 7. *The Finished Mystery.* 1917.

Rutherford, J. F. *Children.*

——. *Creation.*

——. *Deliverance.*

——. *Enemies.*

——. *Government.*

——. *The Harp of God.* 1921.

———. *Jehovah's Witnesses—Why Persecuted?*
———. *The Kingdom.*
———. *"Let God Be True."* 1946.
———. *"Let God Be True."* Rev. ed. 1952.
———. *Light.*
———. *Reconciliation.*
———. *Religion.*
———. *Religious Intolerance—Why?*
———. *Salvation.*
———. *Why Serve Jehovah?*
Theocratic Aid to Kingdom Publishers.
This Means Everlasting Life.
The Truth Shall Make You Free.
The Watchtower, assorted copies.
The Watchtower. December 15, 1949.
The Watchtower. July 1950.
What Has Religion Done for Mankind? 1951.
World Conquest Soon by God's Kingdom. 1955.
You May Survive Armageddon into God's New World.

The following pamphlets are all by J. F. Rutherford and were published by the International Bible Students Association, a subsidiary of the Watchtower Bible and Tract Society. Most of these booklets are out of print.

Angels. 1934.
Armageddon. 1937.
Beyond the Grave. 1934.
Can the Living Talk with the Dead? 1920.
Causes of Death. 1932.
Choosing Riches or Ruin. 1936.
Comfort for the Jews. 1925.
The Crisis. 1933.
Dividing the People. 1933.
Escape to the Kingdom. 1933.
Face the Facts. 1938.
Fascism or Freedom. 1939.
Favored People. 1934.
Final War. 1932.
God and the State. 1941.
Good News. 1932.
Government. 1935.

Government and Peace. 1939.
A Great Battle in the Ecclesiastical Heavens. 1915.
Health and Life. 1932.
Hereafter. 1932.
His Vengeance. 1934.
His Works. 1934.
Home and Happiness. 1932.
Intolerance. 1933.
Judge Rutherford Uncovers the Fifth Column. 1940.
Keys of Heaven. 1932.
The Kingdom. 1932.
The Kingdom, the Hope of This World. 1931.
Liberty. 1932.
The Lost Days. 1928.
Loyalty. 1935.
Millions Now Living Will Never Die. 1920.
Prohibition and the League of Nations. 1920.
Protection. 1936.
Refugees. 1940.
Restoration. 1927.
Righteous Ruler. 1934.
Safety Comfort. 1937.
Supremacy. 1934.
Talking with the Dead. 1920.
Uncovered. 1937.
Universal War Near. 1935.
Warning. 1938.
What Is Truth? 1932.
What You Need. 1932.
Where Are the Dead? 1932.
Who Is God? 1932.
Who Shall Rule the World? 1935.
World Recovery. 1934.

The following books and pamphlets are published by the Dawn Bible Student Association, the official adherents of Pastor Russell.

Armageddon.
Born of the Spirit.
Creation.
The Day of Judgment.
Divine Healing.

Does God Answer Prayer?
Father, Son, and Holy Spirit.
God and Reason.
God's Plan.
His Chosen People.
Hope Beyond the Grave.
Hope for a Fear Filled World.
Jesus the World Saviour.
Our Lord's Return.
Russell, Charles Taze. *Our Most Holy Faith.* 1948.
Spiritualism.
The Truth About Hell.
What Can a Man Pay?
When a Man Dies.
When "Pastor" Russell Died.

Index

Ackley, Maria, 15
Arian heresy, 46, 121
Athanasius, 46
Atonement, Witnesses' teaching of, 30, 32-33, 70-72
Awake, 13 fn.

Baptism, Witnesses' teaching of, 151-52
Benevolence of Witnesses, 107-9
Blood transfusion, Witnesses' teaching of, 94-102
Brooklyn Daily Eagle, 24
Russell's suit against, 15-19
Brooklyn Tabernacle, 14

Christendom, attacks on, 105-15
Clergymen, attacks on, 105-15

Dana and Mantey, 51
Dawn, The, 14
Dawn Bible Students Movement, 13, 14, 102-4
Death, Witnesses' teaching of, 44
Deity of Christ, Witnesses' teaching of, 38-39, 43-68, 133-36, 149

Emphatic Diaglott, The, 48, 49, 56, 59, 65, 70 fn., 93, 156

Finished Mystery, The, 14
"Frank and Ernest," 14, 103

Gilead Missionary Training School, 15 fn., 28
God, Witnesses' teaching of, 29-30, 47-48, 116-28
Government, Witnesses' teaching of, 33, 73-74
Growth of Witnesses, 13-15, 91-92

Hell, Witnesses' teaching of, 33-34, 40, 74-81, 121
Holy Spirit, Witnesses' teaching of, 121-22

Jehovah, the name of, 131-33
Jesus, Witnesses' teaching of, 30, 31, 32, 33

Kingdom, Witnesses' teaching of, 31, 35-36, 87-89, 148, 150-51
Kingdom Farm, 14
Knorr, N. H., 28, 41-42

Man, Witnesses' teaching of, 30, 35, 84-85
Millennial Dawn, 41, 116
"Miracle Wheat" scandal, 16-18, 21

New Birth, Witnesses' teaching of, 146-51
New World Translation of the Greek Scriptures, 129-45

Olin Moyle's suit against Rutherford, 27

Propaganda of Witnesses, 91-94, 154-56

Reason, Witnesses' use of, 116-28
Resurrection, Witnesses' teaching of, 32-33, 39, 69-70
Return of Christ, Witnesses' teaching of, 30-31, 33, 40, 72-73, 139-45
Ross, J. J., 19-23
Russell, C. T., 13-28, 71-72, 91-92, 108
Rutherford, J. F., 14, 19, 25-27, 41-42, 91-92, 108

Satan, Witnesses' teaching of, 30, 31, 34, 80-81
Scripture, Witnesses' teaching of, 24-25, 30, 116-28
Septuagint, 131-32
Sociological aspects of Witnesses, 92

191